Crocheting Soft Toys

Crocheting Soft Toys

Angelika Wolk-Gerche

Floris Books

Translated by Anna Cardwell

Photography by Ulrike & Jürgen Pfeiffer and
Dieter Wolk
Watercolours by Angelika Wolk-Gerche
Diagrams by Ralf Powierski

First published in German as *Krokodil & Kakadu*
by Verlag Freies Geistesleben in 2014
First published in English by Floris Books in 2016

British Library CIP data available
ISBN 978-178250-241-8
Printed in Malaysia

Contents

Clay suction receptacle in the shape of a duck,
Bronze Age Germany, approximately 900 BC.

Wooden crocodile with moveable lower jaw,
Ancient Egypt, approximately 2000 BC.

Fantasy creature made from cloth pieces,
after Gunta Stölzl, Bauhaus, Germany, 1920.

Leather and bead turtle amulet and umbilical-cord
holder, Plains Indians, North America,
nineteenth century.

Introduction

Some time ago I bumped into an old friend in town. She told me, with a sigh, that she'd been looking everywhere for a nice large soft toy for her nephew. But there was nothing! They were all too bright, too kitsch, too bland, badly made or they smelled of chemicals. She had found some high quality animals, but they were few and far between and they were all way over her budget.

Animals have been popular toys for children across all cultures throughout history, made from wood, clay, straw, leather and rags, whatever was to hand, often by the children themselves. Each piece was unique, and children would own only one animal, which made it all the more valuable. Nowadays, soft toys are mass-produced by underpaid workers in faraway countries under questionable conditions. Shelves in children's rooms are full of them. Nevertheless soft toys are relevant playthings, important for role play, comfort, security and emotional support. A soft toy should always be chosen with care – and less is more!

My friend and I sat outside in the sun drinking coffee and exchanging thoughts on the subject. She quickly relaxed and came to a decision…

Her nephew is now the proud owner of a large blue crocheted elephant, with a slight squint but made with love – and unique.

These one-of-a-kind animals are not just for children; they also make special presents for loved ones, best friends, or perhaps for a loved grandparent whose memory is failing but who would appreciate something beautiful to touch.

The Basic
Crochet Stitches

You will only need basic crochet techniques to make the animals in this book, mainly double crochet. Some of the animals require a lot of crocheting, though, so you should practise before attempting to make one. A good toy takes time! You will also need a little imagination and finger dexterity for assembling the animals. It's important to look closely at the photos to ensure you attach each section correctly.

When crocheting in rounds, always mark the start of the row with a contrasting colour yarn. Take a short length of scrap yarn and drape it across the point you want to mark. It will be caught under your next stitch, and you can simply do the same again to mark the next round, moving the marker up when you need to. When you've finished, just pull it out. If you're working

a larger animal in rounds it's best to make a checklist. It's also helpful, particularly for those with less experience, to count the stitches after each round.

Basic crochet techniques

Almost all crochet projects begin with a row of chain stitches, which is the equivalent of casting on in knitting. Chain stitches are also used as a turning stitch at the start of a new row.

You will need to practise maintaining an even tension to make all stitches the same length and not too tight or loose. This gets easier as you gain experience.

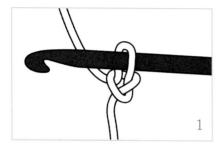

1. First, make a slipknot: make a loop and hold it in place using your less dominant hand, then pull the yarn tail through the loop with your hook. You now have 1 loop on your hook and are ready to start crocheting.

   Hold the tail of the yarn with your less dominant hand, making sure it's taut. As the yarn is at the back of the hook, turn the hook away from you.

2. Now slide the hook under the yarn and turn anticlockwise so the yarn is wrapped around the hook and the hook is pointing down.

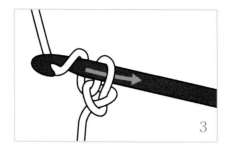

3. Hook the yarn through the slipknot (stitch) on the crochet hook, keeping the yarn taut at all times.

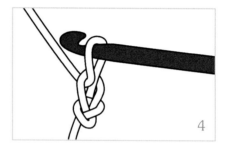

4. Rotate the hook in the opposite direction (clockwise) so the hook is pointing upwards and the new stitch is on the hook.

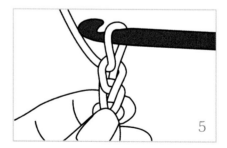

5. Repeat this process to make further chain stitches. After several stitches you will have to gather the stitches closer to the hook with your left hand so the yarn remains taut. Crochet the amount of chain stitches each pattern requires.

Slip stitch

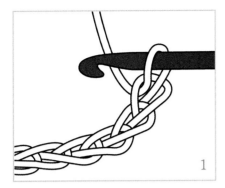

1. Crochet a row of chain stitches plus 1 chain stitch for turning. Insert the hook into the 2nd chain stitch from the hook.

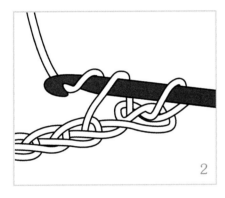

2. Bring the hook behind the yarn so the yarn crosses on top. Rotate the hook anticlockwise to hook the yarn.

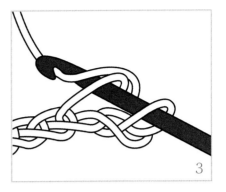

3. Pull the yarn through both loops onto the hook. To continue crocheting slip stitches, insert the hook into the next chain stitch and repeat the process.

Slip stitch is mainly used for joining rows or for forming a ring. It is rarely used for completing an entire project.

Double crochet (US single crochet)

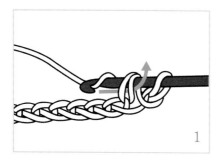

1. Insert the hook into the 2nd chain stitch from the hook, wrap the yarn over the hook and draw through the chain only. You now have 2 loops on your hook.

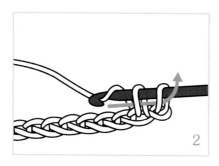

2. Hook the yarn again and draw through both loops. This is the 1st double crochet stitch.

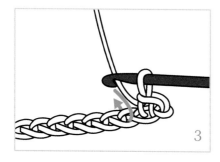

3. Repeat steps 1 and 2 until the row is finished.

Half treble crochet (US half double crochet)

1. Wrap the yarn over the hook and insert it into the desired stitch (here it's the 3rd stitch from the hook). Wrap the yarn around the hook again and pull it through the chain only.

2. Wrap the yarn over the hook and pull through all 3 loops on the hook.

3. The 1st half treble crochet is finished. Repeat steps 1 and 2 until the row is finished.

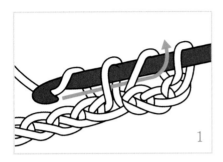

1. Wrap the yarn over the hook and insert it into the desired stitch (here it's the 4th stitch from the hook). Wrap the yarn over the hook again and pull it through the chain only. Wrap the yarn over the hook again and pull it through the 1st 2 loops on the hook.

3. The treble crochet is finished. Repeat steps 1 and 2 until the row is finished.

2. Wrap the yarn around the hook again and pull it through both remaining loops.

13

Decreasing and increasing

To *increase*, double crochet 2 or more stitches into a stitch from the previous row. This is also the way to crochet around a corner. When instructed to 'increase or decrease 5 dc evenly spaced around' make sure the increases or decreases are not placed too close together and not above each other in following rounds.

To *decrease*, skip a stitch from the previous row and continue crocheting as before. Alternatively, for a more even appearance, crochet 1 loop of the next stitch, leave the loop on the hook, crochet the next stitch as you normally would with the loop still on the hook, then draw the yarn through both loops of the 1st and 2nd stitch.

Surface crochet

If you want to crochet a contrasting colour onto your work, you will need an evenly crocheted base, which is best achieved in double crochet. Insert the hook into the gap between the stitches and pull up a loop with the new colour.

Use slip stitches to give the appearance of embroidery chain stitch. Use double crochet to get a raised solid line. You can also crochet other stitch types, as well as points, bows, picots and more to the crocheted fabric.

Embroidery stitches

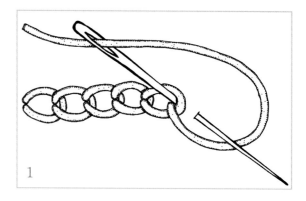

Chain stitch or *slip stitch*. Make sure the thread always remains beneath the needle. Insert the needle back through the hole where it first emerged.

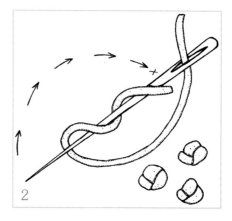

French knot. Push the needle up through the fabric. Keeping the thread taut and flat to the fabric, twist it around the needle. Then insert the needle back into the fabric vertically, just beside the point where it emerged. One twist is sufficient for small knots; larger knots will require two or more twists.

US conversion

UK terms and abbreviations are used for crochet techniques, tools and materials throughout the book, but we have indicated the US equivalents in the opening instructions for each pattern. The main terms that differ are:

Stitches

- Double crochet = US single crochet
- Half treble crochet = US half double crochet
- Treble crochet = US double crochet

Crochet hooks

- 2.5 mm = US C/2 (or B/1)
- 3.5 mm = US E/4
- 6.5 mm = US K/10.5
- 8 mm = US L/11

Abbreviations

- ch = chain stitch
- dc = double crochet
- dec = decrease
- htr = half treble crochet
- inc = increase
- ss = slip stitch
- tr = treble crochet

Finishing Touches

Materials and quantity

Ideally you should choose quality materials when making soft toys for children. You can buy a whole range of natural yarns in beautiful colours. Pure merino wool is soft on the skin and great for working. Pure cotton is also good for crochet, but as it's so smooth and cool to touch, I always combine it with a strand of luxurious, very thin mohair/silk mixed yarn: for example, Schulana Kid-Seta or Mohair Luxe Lang, which are 70% kid mohair/30% silk. The yarn used is listed at the start of each pattern. You can, of course, use other yarns. Use the yardage and crochet hook size as a guideline. Wool shops can usually advise you competently and will show you similar quality yarns to the ones suggested in patterns.

The quantity of materials used is only an approximation as it depends on individual working style. The animals shown in this book have all been crocheted quite tightly. To achieve this you may need to use a size smaller crochet hook than suggested on the yarn label. I prefer tighter stitching for these projects so there are no holes where the stuffing can escape. A looser crochet style will require more wool.

Eyelash yarn is always synthetic (some examples are Schachenmayr Brazilia and Lanartus BEO), so use it sparingly and for specific parts, for example around the wings, ears or as a fringe. Animals made with eyelash yarn are not suitable for children under the age of three as they may swallow the long fibres.

Stuffing material

You can use either unspun sheep's wool or polyester filling to stuff the toys. If you would like an animal made entirely out of natural materials, stuff it with unspun sheep's wool. Some of the soft toys below are designed with a small 'lid' that can be opened to change the stuffing if necessary, for example if the wool felts or lumps after washing. Toys stuffed with polyester filling are easier to wash. Some of the animals pictured here are stuffed with unspun sheep's wool, some with polyester filling.

Regardless which material you decide to use, the correct stuffing technique is important. Use long-fibred sheep's wool so you can stuff with long strands layered over each other rather than lumps or clumps of wool. Tease polyester filling into long strands and insert layer by layer, overlapping.

Allergies and washing

If the recipient of the toy is allergic to dust mites, stuff it with polyester filling. Place the toy in a freezer in a plastic bag every three months to kill off dust mites then carefully wash by hand.

Pure wool is naturally dirt resistant. To maintain a good level of hygiene for a toy stuffed with wool, air in fresh damp air or place outside overnight on a freezing winter night. If you need to wash woollen or cotton toys, wash them by hand in lukewarm water using hand-washing liquid.

Safety

The animals in this book are not suitable for children under the age of three. Even if you choose not to use small parts such as beads (which are rarely used in this book), the toys have small crocheted parts that could come loose and be swallowed. Always sew the parts together well using a double thread stitched twice around. Check the toys from time to time and if necessary sew loose parts back in place. Animals with ears hanging by a thread or with a leg pulled off are a sorry sight and are no good for playing.

Fabric glue

Fabric glue is used to hold everything in place before sewing, not to glue the separate parts to the body. It facilitates sewing and also takes pressure off the seams. Use it sparingly and only when you have determined the correct position of the pieces. Once you've pressed the pieces in place using glue, you will only have a few seconds to adjust them. When the glue is dry you can then sew the pieces without them slipping. I particularly recommend Gütermann textile glue. If you prefer not to use fabric glue, you can pin carefully and sew the pieces in place without it.

Artistic licence

As in all my books, I encourage you to develop your own compositions and use the patterns given here as a guideline. There's no need to adhere exactly to every instruction or detail; your animal will be unique, even if it's squinting, like my friend's elephant described in the introduction.

Large Animal Companions

Elephants

These soft elephants are extremely endearing. Lay them on their backs and, thanks to the method used for sewing together, their legs will flop to the side – inviting children for a cuddle or a quick snooze on their soft bellies.

You will need

- Approximately 250 g (9 oz) light blue or pink fleck 4-ply Regia sock wool (or similar) (yardage: 50 g/210 m or 230 yds) (yarn A)
- Approximately 10 g (½ oz) dark blue or fuchsia yarn (soles and nose discs) (yarn B)
- Small amounts of thin yarn, such as baby wool, sock wool or cotton yarn, for example Schachenmayr Catania, in natural white, dark brown and pink (eyes and mouth) (yarn C)
- Eyelash yarn or similar for fringe (see p.17)
- Approximately 150 g (5 ⅓ oz) unspun sheep's wool or polyester filling for stuffing (see p.18)
- Grey thread, sewing needle, larger needle to sew in yarn tail ends, pins
- Fabric glue if using (see p.18)
- Crochet hooks 3.5 mm and 2.5 mm (US E/4 and C/2 or B/1)

Crochet technique: double crochet (dc) (US single crochet)
Tension/gauge: 22 dc x 22 rounds = 10 x 10 cm (4 x 4 in)
Measurements: approximately 34 cm high (13 ½ in)

Head

Yarn A, double yarn, crochet hook 3.5 mm (US E/4).

Round 1: ch 3 stitches, join with ss to form a ring and crochet 6 dc into the ring.
Round 2: 2 dc into every dc (12 dc).
Round 3: 2 dc into every 2nd dc (18 dc).
Round 4: 2 dc into every 3rd dc (24 dc).
Round 5: 2 dc into every 4th dc (30 dc).
Rounds 6–10: you've made a small disc. This is the basis for most of the patterns in this book. Mark the start of the round with a contrasting colour thread, moving it up as necessary (see p.8). Continue inc by 6 dc per round evenly spaced up to Round 10 (60 dc) (see p.14). This is the widest part of the head!
Rounds 11–26: crochet without inc.
Round 27: dec 4 dc evenly spaced (56 dc).
Round 28: crochet without dec.
Round 29: as Round 27 (52 dc). Crochet the last stitch as ss for a neat finish. Leave a long yarn tail to attach the top of the head.

Stuff the head with 30–40 g (1–1 ½ oz) stuffing material.

Top of the head: crochet a round disc, following the above instructions to Round 9 (54 dc) – ss last stitch. Pull the starting yarn very tight to close the hole and sew the end in well.

Sew the top of the head on with thread very neatly. If necessary you can unpick this seam to renew lumpy or felted stuffing wool after washing and then sew it back in place (see p.18).

Body

Yarn A, double yarn, crochet hook 3.5 mm (US E/4).

Now crochet the body directly onto the finished head. This makes a toy with a firm neck and no slipped stuffing.

Round 1: count the rounds from the bottom, starting with Round 1 in the centre and pick up 48 dc between the 9th and 10th rounds using a new length of yarn. Insert the hook between the stitches, bring up a loop and work a dc, repeat around. The 1st body round, the neck, is finished.

Round 2: 2 dc into every 2nd dc of the previous row (72 dc).

Rounds 3–14: crochet without inc.

Round 15: inc 4 dc evenly spaced around, i.e. 2 dc into 4 dc of the previous round (76 dc).

Rounds 16–19: crochet without inc.

Round 20: as Round 15 (80 dc).

Rounds 21–24: crochet without inc.

Round 25: inc 5 dc (85 dc). This is the widest part of the elephant!

Rounds 26–35: crochet the stomach without inc.

Round 36: now gradually start dec. Dec 5 dc evenly spaced around (80 dc).

Round 37: crochet without dec.

Rounds 38–46: start as Round 36, dec 5 dc (75 dc), then as Round 37, without dec. Continue in this fashion to Round 46 (55 dc).

Round 47: crochet without dec.

Round 48: dec 10 dc (45 dc).

Round 49: crochet without dec.

Round 50: as round 48 (35 dc).

Round 51: crochet without dec. Finished! Leave a long yarn tail.

Stuff the body using approximately 100 g (3 ½ oz) stuffing material.

Make a round disc to close the elephant's bottom, following the instructions for the head to Round 6 (36 dc).

Neatly sew the disc in place. If necessary, you can open it up and re-stuff later.

Trunk

Yarn A, double yarn, crochet hook 3.5 mm (US E/4).

Rows 1–5: ch 15, dc 5 rows. This forms the base of the trunk, which joins neatly to the head. At the end of Row 5, ch 15 and join with ss to the start of Row 5. This makes a ring of chain stitches attached to the rectangle (see photo of trunk opposite).

Rounds 1–7: crochet 7 rounds (30 dc)

Round 8: to taper the trunk, dec 3 dc, evenly spaced on the under side of the trunk (27 dc).

Rounds 9 and 10: crochet without dec.

Round 11: as Round 8 (24 dc).

Rounds 12–14: crochet without dec.

Round 15: as Round 8 (21 dc).

Rounds 16–18: crochet without dec.

Round 19: as Round 8 (18 dc).

Rounds 20–26: crochet without dec.

Rounds 27–29: dec 1 dc per round, evenly spaced and not directly over each other (15 dc).

Rounds 30–33: crochet without dec.

Trunk lip: once Round 33 is complete, turn your work over and dc 5 stitches along the upper side of the trunk. Turn over again and dc 3, turn again and dc 1 to make the lip.

Trunk tip: yarn B

Make a round disc to close the trunk.

Round 1: ch 3, join with ss to form a ring and crochet 5 dc into the ring.

Round 2: 2 dc into every stitch – finished.

Stuff the trunk lightly, shaping it as you stuff.

To attach the disc to the end of the trunk, fold back the trunk a little and sew the disc in place with thread, approximately 2–3 rounds away from the opening.

Ears (x 4)

Yarn A, single yarn, crochet hook 2.5 mm (US C2).

Make each ear out of 2 discs placed over each other and crocheted together. This requires a lot of crocheting, but makes beautiful ears that will not curl at the edges.

Rounds 1–10: make a disc by crocheting in rounds, following the instructions for 'Elephant's Head' on p.23 to Round 10 (60 dc).

Round 11: inc 6 dc evenly spaced around (66 dc).

Round 12: inc 8 dc evenly spaced around (74 dc).

Round 13: as above (82 dc).

Round 14: as above (90 dc).

Earlobes: these are crocheted straight onto the ear discs, in rows back and forth. Inc on one side and dec on the other side to make a slight outward curve. Make sure one earlobe curve is on the right and one on the left so the pieces fit when placed wrong sides facing and sewn together (see photo p.24).

Row 1: 30 dc along one side of ear, turn over.

Row 2: dc until 2nd to last stitch, then 2 dc into this to make outward curve.

Row 3: dc until end of row, but do not crochet final stitch (to keep 30 dc).

Rows 4: as Row 2.

Crochet 14 rows in this fashion.

When all 4 ear pieces are finished, place them over each other wrong sides facing and pin. Crochet around the edge using dc, 2 dc into every stitch at curves and top of earlobes. Put your completed ears aside.

Legs (x 4)

Yarn A, double yarn, crochet hook 3.5 mm (US E/4).

Ch 35, join with ss to form a ring then dc 35 rounds to make a tube – one leg is finished!

Soles (x 4): yarn B

Crochet 4 discs, following the instructions for 'Elephant's Head' on p.23 to Round 5 (30 dc).

Sew the soles very neatly to the leg openings. As the start of the tube is usually slightly tighter than the end, make sure you sew the soles on to the same end for each leg.

Stuff the legs lightly, not more than approximately 6 g (¼ oz) wool per leg (use postal scales for weighing). Make sure the opening of the leg is only lightly stuffed so the joint is not too stiff. Hold the opening flat and sew closed with thread.

Eyes (x 2)

Yarn C in natural white, single yarn, crochet hook 2.5 mm (US C/2).

Round 1: ch 3, join with ss to form a ring and crochet 6 dc into the ring to make a small disc.

Round 2: 2 dc into every dc (12 dc) – this completes the white of the eye.

Make the *pupil* as described above for Round 1 (6 dc) using yarn C in brown.

When all 4 discs are complete, sew the pupils to the whites with thread using small stitches.

Mouth

Using yarn C in pink, ch 6, then dc back and forth, but do not crochet the last stitch of each row. This makes a small triangle. The tip is 1 dc.

Dc twice around 2 sides of the triangle using yarn A. The smiling mouth with lips is finished (see photo p.29).

Tail

Using yarn A, ch 25, then dc 1 row.

Turn then dc to the 15th stitch, ending with ss. This makes a tapered tail.

To finish, cut a few short lengths of yarn (double the length of the tail hair), fold in half and sew to the tip of the tail with a loop (see photo p.24).

Finishing

Your pieces are all finished: the stuffed elephant head and body, stuffed legs sewn shut, ears, loosely stuffed trunk, and eyes, mouth and tail. Check the body from all angles to determine the best side – make this the front.

Use a double sewing thread to sew the pieces together. The thin thread disappears between the crochet stitches and the seams are hardly visible.

First, sew the *ears* to the side of the head.

Fold a small crease in the centre of the ear for shape and sew it in place.

Position the ears at each side of the head, halfway between the front and back of the head. The top of the head should be approximately 1 cm ($^1/_3$ in) above the top of the ears. The bottom of the ears should touch the shoulders (see photo p.22).

Mark the spot determined with a lead pencil or pin. Apply a very thin layer of fabric glue to the edge of the ear and press to the head at the marked spot. You have a few moments to adjust, then pin the ears until the glue dries. Remove pins and sew small, tight stitches around the ear with a double thread, twice around. Children may pull at the ears so a double seam is advisable. The glue allows easier work as nothing will slip.

Count the number of dc from ear to ear to determine the centre of the face and where to position the *trunk* – mark. Count down 6–7 rows from the head seam, making sure the forehead is high and rounded for a childlike expression.

Apply a thin line of fabric glue to the edge of the nose base and press it to the marked spot parallel to a crocheted row. Insert a little stuffing under the nose base and shape. Apply glue to all edges of the nose base and press to the face, making sure the edges don't roll inwards.

Sew the trunk in place with double thread, twice around.

Apply glue sparingly to the back of the *mouth* and press directly under the trunk. The bottom of the mouth should be 1–2 rows above the neck.

To finish, sew the mouth on well with double sewing thread, twice around.

The *eyes* should be placed to the right and left of the trunk, approximately 6–7 rows below the head seam.

To model the face, sew eye sockets. This makes the cheeks and the base of the trunk more distinctive, giving more expression to the face. With double thread or strong thread make a loop in one of the eye sockets so the thread will not slip through. Now push the needle through to the other eye socket and pull to make a hollow. Sew back and forth a few times, pulling the thread tight until the eye sockets are well formed. Sew the thread ends in well. Apply drops of fabric glue to the back of the eyes and press into the sockets. Then sew them in place very carefully with small tight stitches.

There are 1–2 crochet rounds between the neck and the top of the front *legs*.

Make sure you position the seam vertically on the body. Imagine a line running down the body from the ears and place the legs on this line. Pin the front legs in place.

Check whether both legs meet exactly over the centre of the body – this means they are the same length. Once you are satisfied with the position,

apply a line of fabric glue along the seam, press the seam vertically to the body and pin in place until the glue is dry.

Then sew both legs with a double thread and small tight stitches, twice around. The animal is more cuddly if the legs are floppy.

The back legs should be positioned 2 crochet rounds up from the bottom disc and be and in line with the ears and front legs. Make sure they touch the ground because they need to support the elephant when sitting. Pin the leg seams vertically to the body and sit the elephant down to check it sits straight. If you push the soles together they should meet in the centre. Attach them in the same fashion as the front legs.

Sew the *tail* to the rear of the elephant, halfway between the back legs.

For detail, if you like, sew a sparse *fringe* on top of the head using eyelash yarn – finished!

Crocodile

When I first made this crocodile, I was worried it may look too fierce and frightening for children. My grandchild soon put my worries to rest: a crocodile sitting at the end of a bed can never be too fierce; after all, it has to scare away ghosts and monsters!

You will need

- Approximately 180 g (6 ⅓ oz) green merino wool, for example Austermann Merino 105, 100% merino wool (top of body and legs) (yardage: 50 g/105 m or 115 yds) (yarn A)
- Approximately 75 g (2 ⅔ oz) yellow merino wool (underbelly) (yarn B)
- Approximately 20 g (¾ oz) pink yarn (mouth) (yarn C)
- Dark green yarn, for example Schachenmayr Catania cotton (stripes, spikes, claws) (yarn D)
- Yellow yarn, as above (lips, eyes) (yarn E)
- White cotton yarn (teeth)
- Small amount of black yarn (nostrils and pupils)
- 150–200 g (5 ¼–7 oz) unspun sheep's wool or polyester filling for stuffing (see p.18)
- Strong cardboard for reinforcing the mouth (back of a sketchpad)
- Green sewing thread, needles and pins
- Fabric glue if using (see p.18)
- Crochet hooks 3.5 mm and 2.5 mm (US E/4 and C/2 or B/1)

Crochet technique: double crochet (dc) (US single crochet)
Tension/gauge: approximately 21 dc x 23 rows = 10 x 10 cm (4 x 4 in)
Measurements: approximately 70 cm (2 ¼ ft) long

Body and underbelly

Yarn A (back) and B (underbelly) crochet in rows, crochet hook 3.5 mm (US E/4).
The crocodile's green back and yellow underbelly are identical, so you will need to sew this piece twice, once in green and once in yellow. Start with the tip of the tail and dc in rows.

Rows 1–4: ch 4 and dc 4 rows.

Rows 5–16: inc 1 dc at end of each row, that is 2 dc into every 2nd last dc (16 dc).

Rows 17–19: 2 dc into 2nd and 2nd last dc of each row (22 dc).

Rows 20–43: crochet tail without inc.

Rows 44–55: inc 2 dc into every 2nd last dc (34 dc).

Rows 56–63: crochet without inc.

Row 64: inc 1 dc, that is 2 dc into every 2nd last dc (35 dc).

Rows 65 and 66: crochet without inc.

Row 67: as Row 64 (36 dc).

Rows 68 and 69: crochet without inc.

Row 70: as Row 64 (37 dc).

Rows 71–85: crochet shoulders without inc.

Row 86: do not dc last stitch (36 dc).

Rows 87–89: as Row 86 (33 dc).

Row 90: do not dc last and 2nd last stitch (31 dc).

Rows 91 and 92: as Row 90 (27 dc).

Rows 93 and 94: do not dc last stitch (25 dc).

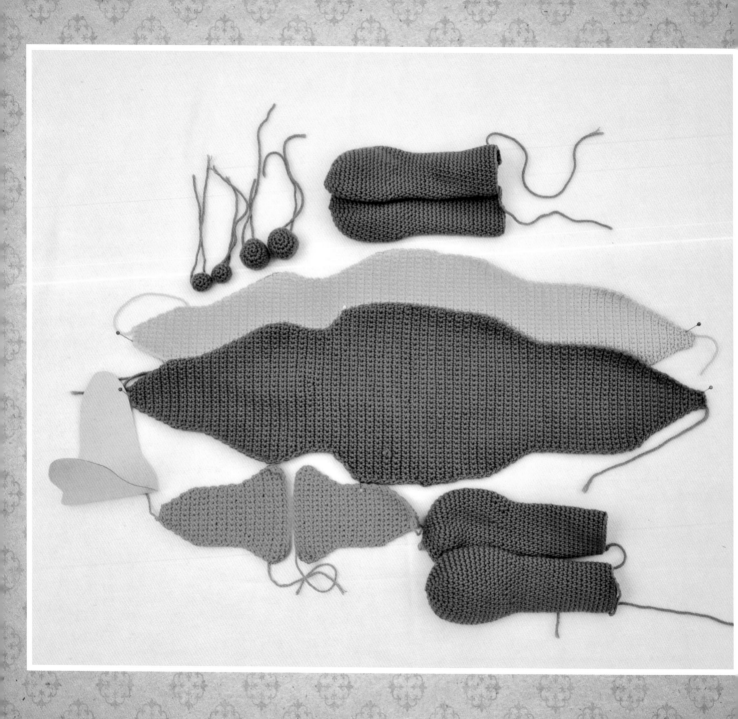

Now crochet the *neck*:

Rows 95–98: continue crocheting without inc.

Rows 99–103: 2 dc into every 2nd last dc (30 dc).

Rows 104–107: crochet without inc.

Rows 108–122: do not dc last stitch (15 dc).

Rows 123–128: dc last stitch again to make the long nose.

Rows 129–138: do not dc last stitch again to make a pointed nose (5 dc).

Half the crocodile's body is finished, weighing approximately 70 g (2 ½ oz). Now crochet the 2nd body piece.

Legs (x 4)

Yarn A, crochet in rounds, crochet hook 3.5 mm (US E/4).

Round 1: ch 3, join with ss to form a ring and crochet 6 dc into the ring.

Round 2: 2 dc into every stitch (12 dc).

Rounds 3–6: continue, following the instructions for 'Elephant's Head' on p.23 to Round 6 (36 dc).

Rounds 7–17: crochet without inc.

Round 18: dec 6 dc evenly spaced around (30 dc).

Round 19: crochet without dec.

Round 20: as Round 18 (24 dc).

Rounds 21–42: crochet without dec to make a tube, the lower leg.

Once all 4 legs are completed, stuff loosely with approximately 20–30 g (³/₄–1 oz) stuffing material each.

   Hold the leg openings closed and dc together with yarn D and crochet hook 2.5 mm (US C2) (12 dc).

   Using the same yarn, crochet *claws*. For each claw, crochet 4 dc then dec to make a triangle by leaving out the edge stitches of each row.

Eyes (x 2)

Round 1: Using yarn A, ch 3, join with ss to form a ring and crochet 6 dc into the ring.

Round 2: 2 dc into every stitch (12 dc).

Round 3: 2 dc into every 2nd stitch (18 dc).

Rounds 4–7: crochet without inc to complete the 1st eye half-sphere.

Stuff firmly.

Nostrils (x 2)

Rounds 1 and 2: follow instructions for 'Eyes' above to Round 2 (12 dc).

Rounds 3 and 4: crochet without inc.

Stuff tightly – finished!

Mouth (x 2)

Yarn C, crochet in rows, crochet hook 3.5 mm (US E/4).

Ch 22 – this is the widest part, the centre of the mouth.

Rows 1–10: dc 10 rows back and forth, without crocheting edge stitches (12 dc).

Rows 11–20: dc 10 rows without dec (12 dc).

Rows 21–27: dc 7 rows without crocheting the final stitch of each row (5 dc).

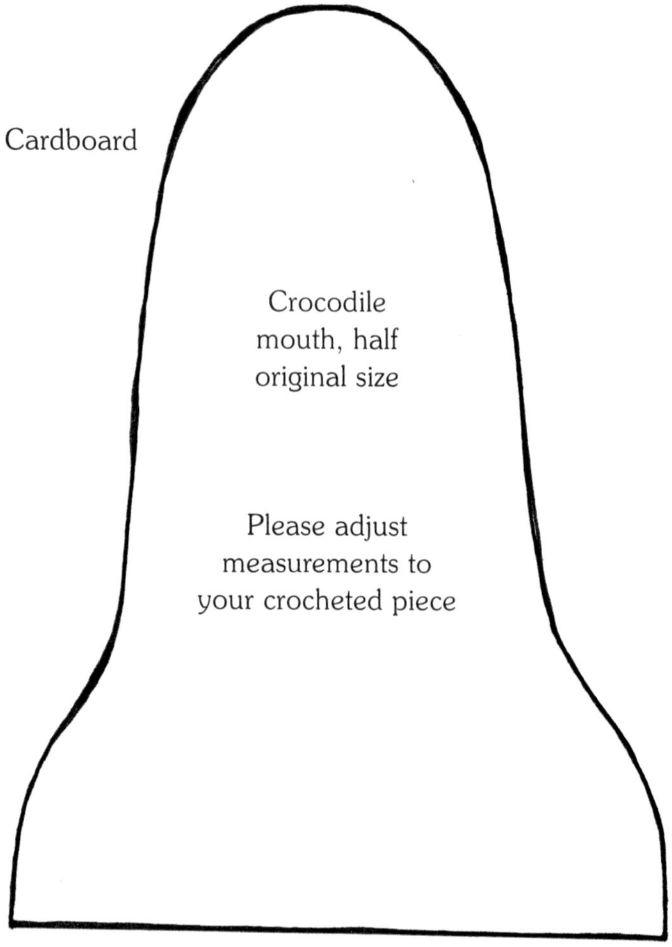

Cardboard

Crocodile
mouth, half
original size

Please adjust
measurements to
your crocheted piece

Mirror image

Finishing

Sew the *mouth* pieces together along the straight edges (back of the mouth). Dc around mouth to make a neat edge.

Cut the mouth reinforcement out of strong cardboard, cutting the top and bottom sections in one piece. Follow the pattern on this page as a guide but use the crocheted mouth for exact measurements. Fold the cardboard in half – with the top and bottom sections over each other. The fold goes at the back of the mouth.

Wrap stuffing material sparingly around the cardboard and wind thread around it to hold in place – this makes an ideal 'fleshy' crocodile mouth.

Place the crocheted mouth pieces over the cardboard jaws. Sew the edges together with pink yarn (yarn C). Wind the yarn around the back of the cardboard a few times to attach it firmly, then put to the side.

Place both *body* parts (underbelly and back) right sides facing and pin. Sew along the edges with tight backstitches up to the mouth. Turn right sides out and smooth the seams.

Check whether the mouth opening is the correct size, adjusting as necessary.

Dc 2 rounds around the mouth opening using green yarn (yarn A).

Stuff the body starting at the tip of the tail. You will need almost all of the remaining stuffing material. Use long thin strands of wool stuffed lengthwise and overlapping to avoid lumps and bumps (see p.18).

Now position the pink *mouth*. Apply a line of fabric glue to the fold (back of the mouth). Push the mouth far into the body, up against the stuffing material.

Now stuff strands of wool from the lower jaw to the back and neck until the crocodile looks good.

When you're satisfied with the stuffing, crochet the mouth in place with 1–2 rounds of dc (yarn A), which makes the lips. You may need to tack the mouth first. Outline the lips with 1 round of dc in light green or yellow (yarn E).

Dc a *side stripe* around the *body* in dark green, using a thinner yarn (yarn D) and crochet hook 2.5 mm (US C/2). Start at the corner of the mouth and crochet to the tip of the tail just above the yellow/green seam.

Fold the *legs* at right angles to make ankle joints. Apply fabric glue to the folds and pin in place. Sew with a double thread and small stitches.

Attach the legs to the sides of the body. The lower legs should touch the ground at the same height as the stomach. Position the tips of the front claws directly under the corners of the mouth (drawing an imaginary vertical line downwards). There should be approximately 8 cm (3 in) between the front and back legs and approximately 25 cm (10 in) from tail tip to rear thighs. Pin the legs in place and check from above whether they are symmetrical. Flatten the inside of the thighs, apply fabric glue sparingly, press, pin and then sew to the body.

Embroider black *nostrils* onto the nose half-spheres using French knots (see p.14). Position them directly beside each other and approximately 5 crochet rows away from the tip of the mouth. Apply a thin layer of fabric glue to the under sides, press to the head and sew in place.

Position the *eyes* close together, approximately 10 cm (4 in) from the nose and 13 cm (5 in) from the tip of the mouth, directly above the corners of the mouth. Attach them in the same way as the nostrils (above) and sew in place well, twice around.

Chain a short length in yellow (yarn E), fold in half to double and then appliqué to the side of the eye circles to make half-shut eyes (see photo p.30). Embroider the pupils over the chain with dark yarn using 2 straight stitches.

If you'd prefer a friendlier crocodile, make round eyes (see for example 'Elephant eyes' p.27).

Now dc the distinct *centre stripe* with dark green (yarn D, see 'side stripe' above) using a 2.5 mm hook. Start at the tip of the tail. The line should end right between the eyes. Mark the centre line with pins as a guide.

Crochet 2 further *stripes* between the first side stripe and the new centre stripe. Begin at the tip of the tail again, dc over the eyes and end between the nostrils. Both lines meet here to make a triangle.

To add *spikes* to the centre line, crochet 6 dc for each spike base. Crochet in rows back and forth, but do not crochet the last dc of each row. This makes a triangle. Crochet smaller spikes as you approach the tail, starting with 5 or 4 dc.

Use white cotton yarn and crochet hook 2.5 mm (US C/2) to crochet the *teeth*. Follow the instructions for back spikes above to create triangles: starting with a base of 6 dc for large; 4 dc for small teeth. Position the teeth in a row approximately 1 cm ($^1/_3$ in) behind the lips.

Your snappy crocodile is finished, measuring over half a metre (2 feet)!

Koala Bears

Koala bears are unquestionably some of the most adorable creatures in the animal world. Is it their unique faces, their secret life in eucalyptus forests or the cute babies they carry around in their pouches that attract us to these magical creatures? It's probably a combination of all three, which make our cuddly koala bear toys truly special.

Mother koala bear

You will need

- Approximately 275 g (9 ¾ oz) light grey wool, for example, Pro Lana Hatnut XL 55, 50% wool, 50% polyamide (yardage: 50 g/55 m or 60 yds) (yarn A)
- Grey eyelash yarn (see p.17) (yarn B)
- Small amount of thin black sock wool or cotton yarn, for example Schachenmayr Catania or Lang Quattro (nose) (yarn C)
- Small amounts of thin yarn (see above) in natural white, brown (eyes) and pink (mouth) (yarn E)
- Approximately 160 g (5 ⅔ oz) unspun sheep's wool or polyester filling for stuffing (see p.18)
- Grey thread, needles and pins
- Fabric glue if using (see p.18)
- Crochet hooks 6.5 mm, 3.5 mm and 2.5 mm (K/10.5, E/4 and C/2 or B/1)

Crochet technique: double crochet (dc) (US single crochet) and chain stitch (ch)
Tension/gauge: 14 dc x 16 rows = 10 x 10 cm (4 x 4 in)
Measurements: sitting animal approximately 28 cm (11 in) high

Head

Yarn A, crochet hook 3.5 mm (US E/4).
Ch 3 and join with ss to form a ring.
Rounds 1–6: follow the instructions for 'Elephant's head' on p.23 to Round 6 (36 dc).
Pull the start yarn tight to close the hole and sew in all yarn ends.
Rounds 7–15: crochet without inc (36 dc).
Round 16: dec 6 dc (see p.14) (30 dc).
Round 17: crochet without dec.
Round 18: as round 16 (24 dc).
Round 19: crochet without dec.
Round 20: as round 16 (18 dc).

Stuff the head through the opening, using approximately 25 g (1 oz) stuffing material.
  Crochet every 2nd dc to close the head opening. This does not look pretty but it will be hidden by the body later. Closing the head completely increases the stability of the finished animal.

Body

Count down 17 rounds from the top of the head.
Round 1: insert the hook into a space between stitches between the 17th and 18th Rounds, pull up a loop and work as dc. Pick up 24 dc around the head in this fashion to make Round 1 of the body (neck). Make sure you always crochet around the outside!
Round 2: 2 dc into every dc (36 dc).
Round 3: crochet without inc.
Round 4: inc 6 dc evenly spaced around (42 dc).
Round 5: crochet without inc.

Round 6: as round 4 (48 dc). This is the widest part of the body.
Rounds 7–22: crochet without inc.
Round 23: now start dec gradually: dec 5 dc evenly spaced around (43 dc).
Round 24: crochet without dec.
Round 25: as round 23 (38 dc).
Round 26: crochet without dec.
Round 27: as round 23 (33 dc).
Round 28: crochet without dec.
Round 29: as round 23 (28 dc).
Round 30: crochet without dec.
Round 31: as round 23 (23 dc).
Round 32: crochet without dec.
Round 33: as round 23 (18 dc).

Stuff the body evenly with approximately 70g (2 ½ oz) stuffing material.

Crochet a separate *bottom* piece to close the opening and sew it in place with neat stitches. This looks good from below and enables the koala to sit securely.
Round 1: ch 3, join with ss to form a ring and crochet 6 dc into the ring.
Round 2: 2 dc into every dc (12 dc).
Round 3: 2 dc into every 2nd dc (18 dc).

Front legs (x 2)

Start with the paws.
Round 1: ch 3, join with ss to form a ring and crochet 6 dc into the ring.
Round 2: 2 dc into every dc (12 dc).
Rounds 3–7: crochet in rounds without inc or dec.
Round 8: inc 3 dc evenly spaced around (15 dc).
Round 9: crochet without inc.
Round 10: as round 8 (18 dc).

Round 11: crochet without inc.
Round 12: as round 8 (21 dc).
Rounds 13–20: crochet without inc. The 1st front leg is finished!

Stuff loosely with approximately 5 g (¼ oz) stuffing material (use a letter scale). Make sure the paw is also stuffed. Sew the opening shut.

Back legs (x 2)

Rounds 1–7: as 'Front legs' above to Round 7 (12 dc). The back legs are slightly fatter than the front legs.
Round 8: inc 5 dc evenly spaced around (17 dc).
Rounds 9–11: crochet without inc.
Round 12: inc 6 dc evenly spaced around (23 dc).
Round 13: crochet without inc.
Round 14: inc 7 dc evenly spaced around (30 dc).
Rounds 15–18: crochet without inc. This makes a rounded thigh.
Round 19: now dec again: dec 5 dc evenly spaced around (25 dc).
Round 20: crochet without dec.
Round 21: as Round 19 (20 dc).
Round 22: crochet without dec.
Round 23: as Round 19 (15 dc).
Round 24: crochet without dec.

Stuff the leg loosely with approximately 10 g (⅓ oz) stuffing material and sew the opening shut.

Ears (x 2)

Yarns A and B, crochet hook 3.5 mm (US E/4).
   Make the ears out of two discs, following the instructions for 'Elephant's head' on p.23 to Round 5 (30 dc) (yarn A).

Fold the ears in half. Crochet the edges together around the semi-circle using eyelash yarn (yarn B), 2 dc into every dc. Crochet 1–2 rows, 2 dc into every dc.

To shape the ears, sew a small fold in the centre of the straight edge.

Eyes (x 2, 2 discs each)

Brown and white yarns, crochet hook 2.5 mm (US C/2).

Crochet a small circle using natural white yarn. Ch 3, join with ss to form a ring and crochet 6 dc into the ring. 2 dc into every dc (12 dc) – the white of the eye is finished.

Make the *pupil* using dark brown yarn. Ch 3 again, join with ss to form a ring and crochet 8 dc into the ring. Ss the last stitch – finished.

Sew the pupil to the white of the eye with thread.

To make the *eyelids*, ch 10 x 2 with natural white yarn and sew directly above the eyes (see photo p.42).

Nose

Yarn C (black), double yarn, crochet hook 3.5 mm (US E/4).
To make the koala's distinctive knobbly nose:
Round 1: ch 3, join with ss to form a ring and crochet 8 dc into the ring.
Round 2: 2 dc in every dc (16 dc).
Rounds 3–5: dc without inc to make a round 'bowl'.

Chin

Yarn A, crochet hook 3.5 mm (US E/4).

Follow the instructions above for the nose, but crochet 1 row less to make it slightly smaller.

Pull the start yarn very tightly to close the hole and sew in the yarn ends well.

Mouth

Chain a string in pink yarn (E) approximately the same length as the chin and nose. Leave approximately 8 cm (3 in) long yarn tails for sewing the mouth in place later (see photo p.38).

Pouch

Yarn A, adding a strand of thin mohair yarn if desired (see 'You will need' p.43 for details) to make the pouch soft and cosy for the baby. Ch 18.
Rows 1–10: crochet in rows back and forth, but do not dc the last stitch of each row.
Rows 11 and 12: do not dc the 2nd last stitch or the last stitch.

Crochet eyelash yarn around the pouch, 2 dc into every dc to make a nice round shape.

Tail

See 'Ears' (p.39) to Row 2 (12 dc), then dc 2 further rows without inc.

Finishing

Check the body from all angles to determine the best side – make this the front.

First, attach the *ears* to the sides of the head. There are 13 stitches between the ears, counting over the top of the head. The top of the head should be approximately 1 cm (1/3 in) higher than the ears. Pin on the *ears*, check the positioning and mark the spot determined.

Apply a line of fabric glue to each ear's folded edge, press to the marked spot, shaping the ear to make it nicely rounded. You have a few seconds to correct before the glue dries.

Sew using double thread; the thin thread will slip invisibly between the crochet stitches and you can work finely and precisely.

Sew the ears in place with small tight stitches, twice around, as the ears need to stay put even when pulled hard!

Next attach the *front legs*. The legs are positioned in line with the ears at the side of the body. There is 1 row between the front legs and neck. Sew the seam vertically to the body.

If desired, glue the legs with some fabric glue first and pin.

Sew on using small stitches and double sewing thread, twice around.

The *back legs* are on the same imaginary line as the ears and front legs. There are approximately 11 stitches between the front and back legs and 2–3 stitches between the thigh and bottom seam.

Pin the back legs in place, making sure they touch the ground and allow the animal to sit straight and stable.

Attach the back legs in the same way as the front legs. They should be closer together, fatter and thus less movable, which is necessary to counterbalance the weight of the pouch and baby koala. It's helpful to glue the larger area to the body before sewing.

Sew the *pouch* to the body, leaving enough space for the baby to fit inside. Position the lower edge of the pouch 9 rows up from the bottom seam.

Next assemble the *face*, starting with the nose. Place the top of the nose 10 stitches down from the top of the head. The forehead should remain nice and rounded. Determine the centre of the face (count the stitches between ears) and mark. Stuff the nose with a little wool to keep it proud. Apply fabric glue very sparingly to the edge, press in place and sew on well.

Attach the chin directly under the nose.

Position the eyes approximately 1 stitch to the right and left of the nose.

Place the mouth chain between the nose and chin. Pull the yarn ends tight and sew in place with matching thread.

To finish, sew the *tail* in place.

The koala's pouch is still empty. Either hide a little surprise in it or make the baby koala on p.43. You could give the baby as a second gift later on.

Baby koala

To make fluffy 'baby fur' (see 'Pouch' p.40), crochet a strand of white mohair/silk yarn together with the cotton yarn.

You will need

- Approximately 25 g (1 oz) light grey cotton yarn, for example Schachenmayr Catania (yardage: 50 g/125 m or 135 yds) (yarn A)
- Small amount of thin white mohair/silk mix yarn, for example Schulana Kid-Seta (yardage: 25 g/210 m or 230 yds) to crochet together with the main yarn (yarn B)
- Grey eyelash yarn, as for 'Mother koala', see p.37 (yarn C)
- Small amounts of thin black yarn, for example Schachenmayr Catania (yardage: 50 g/125 m or 135 yds) (nose)
- Small amounts of brown (eyes) and pink yarn (mouth), as for 'Mother koala' p.37
- Approximately 7 g (¼ oz) unspun sheep's wool or polyester filling for stuffing (see p.18)
- Grey thread and needles
- Crochet hooks 3.5 mm and 2.5 mm (US E/4 and C/2 or B/1)

Crochet technique: double crochet (dc) (US single crochet) and chain stitch (ch)
Tension/gauge: 20 dc x 22 rows = 10 x 10 cm (4 x 4 in)
Measurements: approximately 11 cm (4 ⅓ in) high

Head

Yarn A (combined with yarn B if using), crochet hook 3.5 mm (US E/4).
Crochet in rounds like the mother koala described above.

Round 1: ch 3, join with ss to form a ring and crochet 8 dc into the ring.
Round 2: 2 dc into every dc (16 dc).
Round 3: 2 dc into every 2nd dc (24 dc).
Rounds 4–8: crochet without inc.
Round 9: dec 6 dc evenly spaced around (18 dc).
Round 10: crochet without dec.
Round 11: as Round 9 (12 dc).
Round 12: crochet without dec.

Stuff the head loosely then crochet the opening closed with 1 dc into every 2nd dc. The body will hide this area.

Body

Round 1: count down 10 dc from the top of the head. Insert the hook between stitches between the 10th and 11th rows, pull up a loop and work as dc. Crochet 18 dc.
Round 2: crochet without inc.
Round 3: inc 6 dc evenly spaced around (24 dc).
Round 4: crochet without inc.
Round 5: inc 6 dc evenly spaced around (30 dc).
Rounds 6–10: crochet without inc.
Round 11: dec 6 dc evenly spaced around (24 dc).
Round 12: crochet without dec.
Round 13: as Round 11 (18 dc).
Round 14: crochet without dec.
Round 15: as Round 11 (12 dc).

Stuff the body loosely and crochet shut.

Front leg (x 2)

Ch 3, join with ss to form a ring and crochet 8 dc into the ring.

Crochet 7 further rounds – finished!

Back leg (x 2)

Round 1: ch 3, join with ss to form a ring and crochet 6 dc into the ring.
Round 2: 2 dc into every dc (12 dc).

Crochet a further 8 rounds.

Stuff all 4 legs loosely and sew them shut.

Ears (x 2)

Yarn A (and B if using), crochet hook 2.5 mm (US C/2).
Round 1: ch 3, join with ss to form a ring and crochet 6 dc into the ring.
Round 2: 2 dc into every dc (12 dc).

Crochet eyelash yarn (yarn C) around half the ear.

Sew the ears to the side of the head with the eyelash-yarn side facing out. Leave a high forehead (see photo p.36).

Face

Position the *eyes* between the ears, 7 rows down from the top of the head to make a childlike high forehead, and approximately 4–5 dc apart, leaving space for the nose to fit between them (see photo p.42).

Embroider the eyes in brown yarn using 3 French knots (see p.14) or 3 small, closely placed straight stitches.

Make the round *nose* using black cotton and crochet hook 2.5 mm (US C/2). Ch 3, join with ss to form a ring and crochet 8 dc into the ring. Dc 1 round without increasing.

Make the *chin* using yarn A and crochet hook 2.5 mm (US C/2): ch 3, join with ss to form a ring and crochet 6 dc into the ring – finished.

Position the nose approximately in line with the eyes with the chin directly below. Sew both on well.

Embroider the small *mouth* between nose and chin with a double pink yarn and a straight stitch.

Finishing

Now sew the *legs* in place using a double thread, twice around.

First, sew the front legs to the side of the body in line with the ears, 1 round below the neck. Next sew the back legs in line, 5 rounds further down.

Embroider a small *tail* to the back.

The baby is quite large, so you may have to fold its back legs to squeeze it into the pouch.

Penguins

Penguins are lovable sea birds; the penguin featured here is a king penguin. Penguins can't fly and their waddling gait isn't exactly elegant, but once in water they are very quick and experts at catching fish. Penguins are very caring parents and this one has a baby.

Adult penguin

You will need

- Approximately 65 g (2 $^1/_3$ oz) 4-ply Regia sock wool (or similar) in white with a blue-green fleck, (yardage: 50 g/210 m or 230 yds) (yarn A)
- Approximately 55 g (2 oz) dark blue 100 % merino wool, for example Austermann Merino 105 (yardage: 50 g/105 m or 115 yds) (yarn B)
- Very fine mohair/silk mix yarn for the body, for example, Schulana Kid-Seta or Mohair Luxe Lang (optional) (yarn C)
- Approximately 30 g (1 oz) violet or blue thin cotton yarn, for example Schachenmayr Catania (yardage: 50 g/125 m or 135 yds) (beak, feet and eyes) (yarn D)
- Small amount of thin yellow yarn (eyes, beak outlines, cheek spot).
- Eyelash yarn in grey, black or blue (see p.17) (head tuft)
- Approximately 80 g (3 oz) unspun sheep's wool or polyester filling for stuffing (see p.18)
- Needles, thread and pins
- Soft coloured pencils in yellow and orange
- Black textile pen
- Fabric glue if using (see p.18)
- Crochet hooks 3.5 mm and 2.5 mm (US E/4 and C/2 or B/1)

Crochet technique: double crochet (dc) (US single crochet), chain stitch (embroidery)
Tension/gauge: 20 dc x 20 rows = 10 x 10 cm (4 x 4 in)
Measurements: approximately 28 cm (11 in) high.

Head

Yarn B, crochet hook 3.5 mm (US E/4).
Rounds 1–8: follow the instructions for 'Elephant's head' on p.23 to Round 8 (48 dc).
Rounds 9–17: crochet without inc.
Round 18: dec 6 dc evenly spaced around (42 dc).
Round 19: crochet without dec.
Round 20: as Round 18 (36 dc).
Round 21: crochet without dec.
Round 22: as Round 18 (30 dc).
Round 23: crochet without dec.
Round 24: as Round 18 (24 dc).

Stuff the head with approximately 20 g (¾ oz) stuffing material.

Crochet the opening closed: 1 dc into every 2nd dc. This is not very neat but will be covered by the body later.

Body

Yarn A, double yarn, and crochet together with mohair yarn (yarn C) to make 3 strands if you prefer, crochet hook 3.5 mm (US E/4).
Round 1: count down 24 rounds from the top of the head. Insert your hook between stitches between Rounds 24 and 25, pull up a loop and

work as dc. Crochet 32 dc around the head, making sure you crochet on the outside.

Round 2: dc into every 2nd stitch (48 dc).

Round 3: crochet without inc.

Round 4: inc 5 dc evenly spaced around (53 dc).

Round 5: crochet without inc.

Round 6: as Round 4 (58 dc).

Rounds 7–9: crochet without inc.

Round 10: as Round 4 (63 dc). This makes the plump penguin stomach!

Rounds 11–22: crochet without inc.

Round 23: dec 5 dc evenly spaced around (58 dc).

Rounds 24 and 25: crochet without dec.

Round 26: as Round 23 (53 dc).

Rounds 27 and 28: crochet without dec.

Round 29: as Round 23 (48 dc).

Rounds 30 and 31: crochet without dec.

Round 32: as Round 23 (43 dc).

Round 33: crochet without dec.

Round 34: as Round 23 (38 dc).

Round 35: crochet without dec.

Round 36: dec 10 dc evenly spaced around (28 dc).

Stuff the finished body with approximately 60 g (2 oz) stuffing material.

Crochet a small separate disc to close the opening, following the instructions for 'Head' (see p.47) to Round 4 (24 dc), then carefully sew in place.

Wings (x 4)

2 wings x yarn B, 2 wings x yarn A (under side of the wings), crochet hook 3.5 mm (US E/4).

Rounds 1–7: crochet a round disc, following the instructions for 'Elephant's head' on p.23 to Round 7 (42 dc). This round disc forms the top part of the wings (see left).

Rows 1–5: crochet the lower wing in rows. 12 dc along the edge of the disc. Turn and crochet 12 dc back. Crochet 5 rows in all.

Rows 6–11: do not crochet the final stitch for 6 rows until there are only 6 stitches remaining (6 dc). This makes a tapered wing.

Rows 12–19: crochet without dec for 8 rows (6 dc).

Rows 20–23: do not crochet the final stitch for 4 rows, leaving 2 stitches remaining.

Crochet 4 wings and sew in all yarn ends. Place one dark and one light wing together wrong sides facing, pin and crochet around them with over-edge stitches.

Tailcoat

Yarn B, crochet hook 3.5 mm (US E/4), crochet in rows.

Rows 1–4: ch 20 and dc 4 rows.

Row 5: inc 2 dc approximately in the centre of the piece, 2–3 stitches apart from each other (22 dc).

Rows 6–9: crochet without inc.

Row 10: inc 2 dc (24 dc).

Rows 11–14: crochet without inc.

Row 15: as Row 10 (26 dc).

Rows 16 and 17: crochet without inc.

Row 18: as Row 10 (28 dc).

Row 19: crochet without inc.

Rows 20–32: you are now at the centre of the back (see left). Start dec gradually: do not crochet the edge stitch at the end of each row until 15 dc remaining in Row 32. This is the base of the tail; now crochet the tail itself.

Tail: do not crochet the edge stitch at the end of each row until 4 dc remaining at the tip of the tail.

Crochet the light under side of the tail in the same way. Ch 15 and dc in rows back and forth, dec by 1 stitch at the end of each row until 4 dc remain at the tip of the tail.

Crochet the tail parts together in the same way as the wings.

Smooth down the tailcoat and wings ready to sew together. Sew the wings to the tailcoat approximately 7 cm (2 ¾ in) along the top curve, leaving the rest of the wing free to move (see photo p.55).

Beak

Yarn D, crochet hook 2.5 mm (US C/2), crochet in rounds.
Ch 12 and join with ss to form a ring.
Rounds 1–4: dc 4 rounds.
Round 5: dec 2 dc evenly spaced around (10 dc).
Rounds 6–8: crochet without dec.
Round 9: as Round 5 (8 dc).
Rounds 10–12: crochet without dec.
Round 13: as Round 5 (6 dc).
Round 14: crochet without dec.

Crochet the remaining opening closed with 1 dc.
Stuff the beak firmly, particularly at the tip, using a pencil or similar to help.

Feet (x 2)

Yarn and crochet hook as 'Beak' above.
Round 1: crochet a round disc to make the heel: ch 3, join with ss to form a ring and crochet 6 dc into the ring.
Rounds 2–4: follow the instructions for 'Elephant's head' on p.23 to Round 4 (24 dc).
Crochet a further 21 rounds without inc.

Stuff the feet loosely and smooth down, particularly around the opening.

Work 3 toes while crocheting the opening closed: crochet 4 dc, turn, crochet 3 dc, turn, crochet 2 dc, turn again, crochet 1 dc. This triangle is the 1st toe.

Once all 3 toes are finished, dc 1 row to outline, inc by 2 dc at the tip of each toe.

Eyes (x 2)

Yarn D, crochet hook 2.5 mm (US C/2).
Round 1: ch 3, join with ss to form a ring and crochet 6 dc into the ring.
Round 2: 2 dc into every dc (12 dc) – finished!

Draw on black pupils with a textile pen.

Cheek spots (x 2)

Round 1: ch 3 stitches, join with ss to form a ring and crochet 6 dc into the ring.
Round 2: 2 dc into every dc (12 dc).
Now crochet in rows. Crochet 4 dc to the edge of the circle, turn, 4 dc back. Continue in this fashion without crocheting the edge stitch until 1 dc remains. Crochet an additional dc to the tip.

Finishing

First, sew the *tailcoat with wings* to the body. Lay the tailcoat on the neckline, so you can't see any light body wool peeking through. Stroke and smooth the tailcoat and wings around the body. Apply a line of fabric glue to the neck and press in place well. Then pin in place. The glue stops everything slipping and makes sewing easier later.

Sew with a double sewing thread and small neat stitches. First, sew the tailcoat along the neckline and shoulders to the wings. Then sew the tailcoat to the back, starting where the wings and the tailcoat meet down to the start of the tail (approximately 7 cm, 2 ¾ in on each side). Leave the tail and wings free to move.

Position the *feet* so the penguin can stand well, then pin. Check the tail tip is exactly between the closely placed heels. The toes can be turned outwards.

Glue the feet with a drop of textile glue to the determined spot. You can only adjust the feet for a few seconds before the glue dries. Stand the penguin up on its feet straight away. Sew the feet on with double thread and small stitches all the way around.

Now make the *face*. Crochet yellow ss around the beak, taking care to crochet exactly over the tip (see right and overleaf).

Hold the beak to the face and check the positioning, leaving enough space for a nice high forehead. Once you're satisfied with the position apply fabric glue sparingly to the beak and press it to the face. Position the eyes approximately 11 rows up from the neck, approximately 11 stitches apart to the left and right of the beak. Mark the spot with pins.

Attach a double thread to a pinned eye spot, push the needle through face to the other eye spot and pull the thread tight. Then sew back again. Repeat this process 2–3 times to make eye sockets. This models the face and makes it more expressive. Sew the thread tails in well.

Apply a drop of fabric glue to each eye disc and press into the eye sockets. Pin and sew the eyes and beak in place with small stitches and double thread.

To brighten the eyes and the penguin's facial expression, embroider a row of bright yellow chain stitches around them.

Sew the cheek spots well in place.

Embroider a few strands of *eyelash yarn* to the top of the head.

Crochet around the wings and base of body directly above the feet with eyelash yarn, if desired (see photo below).

Use coloured pencils for *neck colouring*. Hold the pencils at an angle and shade under the neck to colour. Continue down the stomach with the yellow pencil, gradually fading the colour.

Baby penguin

You will need

- Approximately 20 g (¾ oz) thin natural white wool (yardage: 100 g/420 m or 460 yds) (yarn A)
- White mohair/silk mixed yarn, for example Schulana Kid-Seta or similar (yarn B)
- Dark blue Merino wool (you can use the leftover yarn from the large penguin, see yarn B p.47) (yarn C) (cap)
- Violet thin cotton yarn (see large penguin p.47, yarn D) (feet and beak)
- White eyelash yarn (see p.17)
- Some unspun sheep's wool or polyester filling for stuffing (see p.18)
- Thread, needles and pins
- Fabric glue if using (see p.18)
- Crochet hooks 3.5 mm and 2.5 mm (US E/4 and C/2 or B/1)

Crochet technique: double crochet (dc) (US single crochet); chain stitch (ch); half treble crochet (htr) (US half double crochet)
Tension/gauge: 22 dc x 20 rows = 10 x 10 cm (4 x 4 in)
Measurements: approximately 12 cm (4 ¾ in) high

Head

Crochet with 3 yarn strands: 1 x yarn A, 2 x yarn B and crochet hook 3.5 mm (US E/4).
Rounds 1–4: follow the instructions for 'Elephant's head' on p.23 to Round 4 (24 dc).
Rounds 5–9: crochet without inc.
Round 10: dec 4 dc evenly spaced around (20 dc).
Round 11: dec 5 dc evenly spaced around (15 dc).
Stuff the head loosely.
Round 12: dec 6 dc evenly spaced around (9 dc).

Body

Round 1: count 11 rounds down from the top of the head. Insert the hook between stitches and between Rounds 11 and 12, pull up a loop and work as dc. Dc 16 in this way around the head.
Round 2: 2 dc into every 2nd dc (24 dc).
Round 3: crochet without inc.
Round 4: inc 8 dc evenly spaced around (32 dc).
Rounds 5–10: crochet without inc, to make the round stomach.
Round 11: dec 4 dc evenly spaced around (28 dc).
Round 12: crochet without dec.
Round 13: dec 4 dc evenly spaced around (24 dc).
Round 14: crochet without dec.
Round 15: dec 6 dc evenly spaced around (18 dc).

Stuff the body loosely.

Bottom

Crochet a disc as for the head to Round 3 (18 dc). Sew the lid neatly to the body.

Cap

Rounds 1–4: using yarn C, crochet a disc as for the head to Round 4 (24 dc).
Round 5: crochet without inc.
Round 6: 2 dc into every 4th dc of the previous round (30 dc).
Rounds 7–10: crochet without inc.

Now crochet the small *forehead triangle* (see photo p.52) in rows back and forth: dc 4, turn, dc 3, turn, dc 2.

Ch 2–3 stitches to the tip to connect to the beak later.

Wings (x 2)

Crochet with 2 yarn strands: 1 x yarn A, 1 x yarn B, in rows, using eyelash yarn for joining.

The wings are made from 2 small triangles folded in half: ch 10 and dc 2 rows.

Continue crocheting in rows back and forth, but do not crochet the last stitch; this creates a triangle.

Fold the triangle in half lengthwise and crochet together with a length of eyelash yarn – finished!

Beak

Yarn D, crochet hook 2.5 mm (US C/2).

Ch 2, join with ss to form a ring and crochet 6 dc into the ring.

Dc 1 round, then pull the start yarn very tight to close the hole and sew the yarn ends in well – this is the tip of the beak.

Feet (x 2)

Yarn D, crochet hook 2.5 mm (US C/2).
Round 1: ch 3, join with ss to form a ring and crochet 6 dc into the ring.
Round 2: 2 dc into every stitch (12 dc).
Crochet a further 11 rounds – the 'foot tube' is finished.

Stuff the tubes loosely and stroke flat.

Crochet the openings closed with a row of dc. At the same time make 3 toes using htr (see p.12).

Tail

Yarn A, crochet hook 2.5 mm (US C/2).

The tail is a small triangle. Ch 6 and continue as for the wings.

Finishing

Attach the *wings* to the side of the body, with the eyelash-yarn side pointing down and the top side approximately 2 stitches from the neck. Attach the wings with fabric glue, pin in place and sew with double thread, twice around.

Once the wings are in place you can determine the centre of the face and the position of the *beak*. Mark with a pin.

Pull the *cap* over the head. The tip of the small triangle should end exactly at the marked beak point. If necessary, remove or add a dc so it fits! Pull the yarn tail down and sew it in to attach the tip. Then sew right around the cap with thread.

Glue the *beak* to the forehead triangle and sew in place.

Sew short straight stitches to the left and right of the beak to make a slight smile.

To finish, embroider French-knot *eyes* (see p.14) below the brows of the cap (see photo p.52).

Cockatoo

This young cockatoo, with its large head and feet, is stuffed loosely and is very cuddly. The soft 'baby down' and light lustre of the 'feathers' are created by adding a strand of mohair yarn to the cotton.

You will need

- Approximately 110 g (4 oz) cotton yarn, for example Style Magicline Anchor, in pink with coloured flecks (yardage: 50 g/70 m or 75 yds) (yarn A)
- Approximately 40 g (1 ½ oz) thin pink mohair/silk mix yarn, for example Schulana Kid-Seta or Mohair Luxe Lang (yardage: 25 g/175–210 m or 190–230 yds) (yarn B)
- Approximately 30 g (1 oz) cotton yarn in white or light pink (under side of wings and tail) (yarn C)
- Approximately 20 g (¾ oz) apricot or orange cotton yarn, for example Polo Zitron (yardage: 50 g/140 m or 155 yds) (beak and feet) (yarn D)
- Approximately 20 g (¾ oz) pink eyelash yarn (see p.17)
- Small amounts of black, beige and pink thin sock wool or cotton yarn, for example Schachenmayr Catania (eyes and around the tail)
- Approximately 80 g (3 oz) unspun sheep's wool or polyester filling for stuffing (see p.18)
- Pink thread, needles, pins
- Fabric glue if using (see p.18)
- Crochet hooks 3.5 mm and 2.5 mm (US E/4 and C/2 or B/1)

Crochet technique: double crochet (dc) (US single crochet); chain stitch (ch); picots

Tension/gauge: 16 dc x 18 rows = 10 x 10 cm (4 x 4 in)
Measurements: approximately 25 cm (10 in) high, without head tuft

Head

Yarn A, adding a yard of yarn B for lustre, crochet hook 3.5mm (US E/4).

Rounds 1–7: follow the instructions for 'Elephant's head' on p.23 to Round 7 (42 dc).
Rounds 8–15: crochet without inc.
Round 16: dec 6 dc evenly spaced around (36 dc).
Round 17: crochet without dec.
Round 18: as Round 16 (30 dc).
Round 19: crochet without dec.
Round 20: as Round 16 (24 dc).
Round 21: crochet without dec.
Round 22: as Round 16 (18 dc).

Stuff the head with approximately 18–20 g (¾ oz) stuffing material.

Crochet the opening closed, with 2 dc into every 2nd dc. This doesn't look very neat but it will be covered by the body.

Body

Round 1: count down 19 rows from the top of the head. Insert the hook between the stitches between Rounds 19 and 20, pull up a loop and work as dc. Crochet 30 dc around the head, being careful to always crochet around the outside.
Round 2: work 2 dc into every 2nd dc (45 dc).

Round 3: crochet without inc.

Round 4: inc 5 dc evenly spaced around (50 dc).

Rounds 5–15: crochet without inc. This is the stomach and fattest part of the cockatoo. Attach a thread to the start of the rounds.

Round 16: dec 5 dc evenly spaced around (45 dc).

Rounds 17–23: crochet without dec.

Round 24: as Round 16 (40 dc).

Rounds 25–27: crochet without dec.

Round 28: as Round 16 (35 dc).

Round 29: crochet without dec.

Round 30: dec 10 dc evenly spaced around (25 dc).

Stuff the body evenly with approximately 60 g (2 oz) stuffing material.

Crochet the opening closed with 1 dc into every 2nd dc. Later the feet will cover this area.

Wings (x 4)

Each wing has a darker upper side (yarn A/B) and a lighter under side (yarn C), both made in the same way, using crochet hook 3.5mm (US E/4).

Rounds 1–6: crochet a disc, following the instructions for 'Elephant's head' on p.23 to Round 6 (36 dc).

Row 1: start crocheting the tapered wing tips straight onto this circle (see left): turn, dc 12 (12 dc).

Row 2: turn, dc 12 (12 dc).

Rows 3–10: dc 8 rows without crocheting the last stitch of each row, to make a triangle (4 dc).

Rows 11–16: crochet 6 rows without dec (4 dc)

Rows 17–19: crochet without dc the last stitch of each row until 1 dc remaining – this is the wing tip.

Match the upper sides to the under sides and pin together, wrong sides facing. Dc around the wings using eyelash yarn to join them together, starting 2 or 3 dc into the wing tip, so it doesn't pucker.

Tail (x 2)

The tail has a darker upper side (yarn A/B) and a lighter under side (yarn C), both made in the same way, crocheted in rows using crochet hook 3.5 mm (US E/4).

Rows 1–13: ch 8 and dc 13 rows.

Row 14: inc 1 dc at the beginning and end of the row: that is, 2 dc into 2nd dc and 2nd last dc.

Rows 15–19: dc 5 further rows without inc.

Crochet 1 additional row to the tail's under side so it peeks out from under the top side.

Crochet picots to the bottom edge to make feathers (see photo p.61): ch 3, crochet 1 dc into 3rd stitch from hook, then 1 dc to the bottom edge of the tail piece – the 1st feather is finished. Ch 3 again and repeat as above until you reach the end.

Place the tail parts together wrong sides facing and crochet together with a matching yarn.

Crochet picots (or small chain loops if you prefer) to the upper side of the tail to make more feathers.

Feet (x 2)

Yarn D, crochet hook 3.5 mm (US E/4).

Each foot is comprised of 4 toes. Crochet 8 tubes in rounds, closed at one end, open at the other end (see left).

Ch 3, join with ss to form a ring and crochet 8 dc into the ring.

Now dc 15 rounds. The 1st toe is finished. Pull the start yarn tight to close hole and sew the yarn end in well.

Once all the 8 toes are finished, loosely stuff them right to their tips and sew the opening closed with thread.

Apply fabric glue sparingly to the seams and gather 4 toes together with 3 toes pointing to the front and 1 toe to the back, glued seams touching. Once the glue is dry, sew the toes together with needle and thread using small tight stitches. Repeat for the 2nd foot.

Beak

Using yarn D, ch 14, join with ss to form a ring and dc 3 rounds – this forms the base of the beak (see photo p.58).

Crochet a row of 7 dc onto the base ring.

Dc back and forth without dc the last stitch of each row until 1 dc remains.

Join the tip to the base and sew in the yarn tail to make a beak.

Crest (x 4)

Use the same yarn as the body (yarn A/B) to make the crest in 4 parts.

Crochet 4 small triangles in rows: ch 7 then dc back and forth without dc the last stitch of each row until 1 dc remains.

Crochet eyelash yarn around 2 sides of each triangle.

Eyes (2 x 2 discs each)

Use beige and black yarns, crochet hook 2.5 mm (US C/2).

Round 1: using beige yarn, ch 3, join with ss to form a ring and crochet 6 dc into the ring.

Round 2: 2 dc into every dc.

To make the pupil out of black yarn, crochet Round 1, then sew the black disc to the beige disc with thread.

Finishing

Examine the body from all angles to determine the best side – make this the front. Now attach the *wings*. Position them at the side of the body, slightly further towards the back, exactly at the neckline. There should be approximately 17 dc between the wings at the front and approximately 12 dc around the back. Apply a line of fabric glue sparingly to approximately 8 cm (3 in) of the top of the wing (leaving the rest free), press to the body and pin. Sew in place with double thread and small stitches, twice around.

Position the *beak* in the centre of the face, approximately 5 rounds up from the neck. Apply fabric glue to the edge of the beak and sew in place carefully.

The lower edges of the *eyes* are approximately 7 rounds up from the neckline, with approximately 9 dc between the eyes (counted over the beak). Mark the position of each eye with pins, then sew eye sockets to give the face more expression before attaching the eyes. Remember to take into account when marking the eye positions

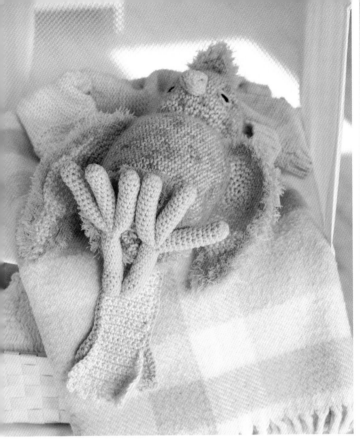

that the distance between the eyes will decrease after making the eye sockets; the eyes should not be too close together or the face will not be so friendly. Attach a double thread and needle to an eye spot and push the needle through to the other eye spot. Pull the thread tight to make an indentation, push the needle through to the other eye spot and pull tight again. Repeat this process 2–3 times to make stable eye sockets. Sew the yarn tails in well. Sew the eyes on well.

Count 7 rounds up from the beak to find the position of the 1st *crest* triangle. Sew all 4 triangles behind each other approximately 4 dc apart.

Sew the magnificent double *tail* in the centre of the back, between the wings, approximately 20 rounds down from the neck. Only attach the top edge.

Pin the *feet* in place and check whether the bird can stand firmly. Place both feet closely together, with the back claw sticking out approximately 3.5 cm (1 ⅔ in) at the back.

Pat the bird's bottom flat and apply fabric glue sparingly to the top of the claws. Stand the cockatoo up immediately. Once the glue is dry sew everything in place well with needle and double thread.

To finish, dc around the bottom of the body with eyelash yarn – so the claws peek out under some soft pink feathery down.

Pig

This pig is crocheted using two different strands of yarn: a smooth cotton and a luxurious mohair/silk mix, which captures the soft, silky sheen of a piglet's skin very well. It makes a lovely toy for children to stroke.

You will need

- Approximately 120 g (4 ¼ oz) pink cotton yarn, for example Schachenmayr Catania (yardage: 50 g/125 m or 135 yds) (yarn A)
- Approximately 80 g (3 oz) apricot mohair/silk mix yarn, for example Schulana Kid-Seta or similar (yardage: 25 g/210 m or 230 yds) (yarn B)
- Approximately 20 g (¾ oz) grey or beige cotton yarn, for example Schachenmayr Catania (trotters) (yarn C)
- Small amounts of white and blue cotton yarn (eyes) (yarn D)
- Small amount of pink yarn, for example baby wool (mouth) (yarn E)
- Small amount of brown yarn (nostrils)
- Approximately 120 g (4 ¼ oz) unspun sheep's wool or polyester filling for stuffing (see p.18)
- Pink and white sewing thread, sewing needles and pins
- Fabric glue if using (see p.18)
- Crochet hooks 3.5 mm and 2.5 mm (US E/4 and C/2 or B/1)

Crochet technique: double crochet (dc) (US single crochet)

Tension/gauge: 20 dc x 22 rows = 10 x 10 cm (4 x 4 in)

Measurements: sitting pig approximately 27 cm (10 ½ in) high

Head

Use 3 strands of yarn: 1 x yarn A, 2 x yarn B. Crochet hook 3.5 mm (US E/4).

Rounds 1–7: follow the instructions for 'Elephant's head' on p.23 to Round 7 (42 dc).

Round 8: inc 8 dc evenly spaced around (50 dc). Mark the start of the round with a contrasting coloured length of yarn (see p.9).

Rounds 9–18: crochet without inc.

Round 19: dec 6 dc evenly spaced around (44 dc).

Round 20: crochet without dec.

Round 21: as Round 19 (38 dc).

Round 22: crochet without dec.

Round 23: as Round 19 (32 dc).

Round 24: dec 8 dc (24 dc), ss last stitch, leaving a long yarn tail.

Stuff the head with approximately 25 g (1 oz) stuffing material.

Top of the head: follow the instructions for 'Elephant's head' on p.23 to Round 4 (24 dc).

Sew the lid in place very carefully using the long yarn tail.

Unpick the seam if necessary to re-stuff the pig after washing if the stuffing wool becomes lumpy or felted (see p.18).

Body

Yarn and hook as for 'Head' above.

Round 1: count up 7 rows from the 1st head round. Insert the hook between stitches and between Rounds 7 and 8, pull up a loop and work as dc. Crochet 40 new dc around the head, remembering to crochet on the outside!

Round 2: 2 dc into every 2nd dc (60 dc) to make the shoulders. Mark the start of the round with a contrasting colour yarn.

Rounds 3–10: crochet without inc.

Round 11: inc 5 dc evenly spaced around (65 dc).

Round 12: crochet without inc.

Round 13: as Round 11 (70 dc).

Round 14: crochet without inc.

Round 15: as Round 11 (75 dc). This is the widest part of the body!

Rounds 16–25: crochet without inc.

Round 26: dec 5 dc evenly spaced around (70 dc).

Round 27: crochet without dec.

Round 28: as Round 26 (65 dc).

Round 29: crochet without dec.

Round 30: as Round 26 (60 dc).

Round 31: crochet without dec.

Round 32: as Round 26 (55 dc).

Round 33: crochet without dec.

Round 34: as Round 26 (50 dc).

Round 35: crochet without dec.

Round 36: as Round 26 (45 dc).

Round 37: crochet without dec.

Round 38: dec 10 dc evenly spaced around (35 dc). Leave a long yarn tail for sewing the lid in place.

Stuff the body evenly without holes or lumps using approximately 75 g (2 ⅔ oz) of stuffing material.

Make a round disc to close the pig's bottom, following the instructions for 'Elephant's head' on p.23 to Round 4 (24 dc). Ss the last stitch, sew in the yarn tail and sew the disc carefully to the body. If required, you can unpick the seam to change stuffing if the wool becomes lumpy or felted after washing.

Legs and trotters (x 4)

Yarns A/B, as above, and yarn C, double yarn, crochet hook 3.5 mm (US E/4).

Ch 25, join with ss to form a ring and dc 20 rounds.

Crochet the trotters to the legs using light grey or beige yarn (yarn C), double yarn. Dc 3 rounds – one leg tube is finished.

Yarn C, single yarn, crochet hook 2.5 mm (US C/2).

Make small discs for the trotter *soles* following the instructions for 'Elephant's head' on p.23 to Round 5 (30 dc).

Sew the soles neatly to the trotter openings.

Stuff the legs loosely with a little stuffing material, very sparingly at the top so the joint are nice and loose, and sew closed with thread.

Ears (x 2)

Yarns A/B, crochet hook 3.5 mm (US E/4), crochet in rows.

Row 1: ch 12 and dc 1 row. This is the starting edge of the ear.

Rows 2–8: 2 dc into every last stitch (19 dc).

Rows 9 and 10: crochet without inc. This is the centre and widest part of ear.

Rows 11–14: do not dc the last stitch for 4 rows (15 dc).

Rows 15–20: dec 2 dc per row: do not dc 2nd last and last dc until you have 3 dc remaining.

Row 21: turn and crochet 1 dc to make the tip of the ear.

Now dc around the ear for a neat edge, with 2 dc in the corner stitch to avoid puckering.

Eyes (x 2, 2 discs each)

White and blue cotton yarn, crochet hook 2.5 mm (US C/2).

Ch 3 in white, join with ss to form a ring and crochet 9 dc into the ring. Crochet tightly!

Make the pupil in blue yarn in the same way but with 6 dc in the ring.

Sew the pupil to the white disc with thread, leaving only a thin white edge visible.

Snout and mouth

Yarns A/B, crochet hook 3.5 mm (US E/4).

Start the snout with a rectangular base that joins to the forehead (see photo p.64): ch 6, then dc 5 rows back and forth.

Ch 15 from the end of the rectangle and join to the start of rectangle with ss to form a ring.

Dc 5 rounds – complete!

Yarn E, crochet hook 2.5 mm (US C/2).

Make a disc to close the snout, following the instructions for 'Elephant's head' on p.23 to Round 5 (30 dc).

Crochet the laughing mouth (see photo p.67) using hook and yarn as above: ch 6 then dc in rows back and forth, without dc each final stitch to make a small triangle.

Crochet around the triangle twice, using Yarns A/B and crochet hook 3.5 mm (US E/4) to make lips.

Curly tail

Ch 30, turn, crochet 1 dc into every 2nd dc – finished!

Finishing

Attach the *ears* first. Fold or roll them in from the sides and sew approximately 2 cm (¾ in) up from the ear base (see photo p.67).

Examine the body from all angles to determine the best side – make this the front. Count 4 rounds down from the seam at the top of the head and approximately 16–17 dc apart around the front of the head. The fold openings face mainly down and slightly to the front. First, pin the ears in place, and when you're satisfied with the position, mark the spots with a lead pencil.

Apply fabric glue sparingly to the edges of the folded ears and press them quickly to the marked spots. Let the glue dry for a few minutes. Use a double thread to sew the ears on with small tight stitches, twice around.

Attach the *legs* following the instructions for 'Elephant' on p.28.

Embroider 2 French knots (see p.14) to the *snout* disc with dark brown yarn to make nostrils.

Apply fabric glue very sparingly to the edge of the nose disc and place it directly onto the snout. Sew the disc to the snout from below with very small stitches, leaving a slightly raised edge like a real piglet.

Stuff the snout loosely.

To attach the snout, first pin the forehead rectangle in place, approximately 6 dc down from the seam at the top of the head and exactly between the ears (count the stitches to determine the centre). Apply fabric glue to the edge of the rectangle and press in place.

Stuff some stuffing material into the rectangle, pinch the base of the snout together with thumb and forefinger so it bulges slightly, and sew firmly in place with double thread, twice around.

Apply glue sparingly to the back of the *mouth* and press directly under the snout. The bottom of the mouth should be 1–2 rows above the neck.

Sew the mouth on well with double sewing thread, twice around.

Position the *eyes* directly beside the snout just where it starts to protrude, approximately 9 rows down from the head seam.

If desired, outline the eyes with eyelashes (straight stitch).

To finish, you can knot a few strands of mohair to the lid seam as a *fringe*.

Sew the curly *tail* at the centre of the pig's bottom.

Sheep

This soft lovable sheep is made out of an unusual but beautiful material: bumpy spun bouclé wool and black yak wool, from a Himalayan cow. Cuddling her will surely give you sweet dreams.

You will need

- Approximately 140 g (5 oz) bouclé sheep's wool, for example Rowan Purelife, 100% wool (yardage: 100 g/60 m or 65 yds) (yarn A)
- Approximately 45 g (1 ½ oz) black yak/merino wool mix, for example Lang YAK, 50 % yak, 50 % merino wool (yardage: 50 g/130 m or 140 yds) (yarn B)
- Small amounts of thin white, brown and pink sock wool, baby wool or cotton yarn, for example Schachenmayr Catania (eyes and mouth)
- Approximately 70 g (2 ½ oz) unspun sheep's wool or polyester filling for stuffing (see p.18)
- Brown and natural white thread, needles and pins
- White coloured pencil or tailor's chalk
- Fabric glue if using (see p.18)
- Crochet hooks 8 mm, 3.5 mm and 2.5 mm (US L/11, E/4 and C/2 or B/1)

Crochet technique: double crochet (dc) (US single crochet)

Tension/gauge: 24 dc x 22 rows = 10 x 10 cm (4 x 4 in) (yarn B); 10 dc x 9 rows = 10 x 10 cm (4 x 4 in) (yarn A)

Measurements: approximately 27 cm (10 ½ in) high

Head

Yarn B, crochet hook 3.5 mm (US E/4).

Round 1: starting at the nose, ch 3, join with ss to form a ring and crochet 6 dc into the ring.

Rounds 2–5: follow the instructions for 'Elephant's head' on p.23 to Round 5 (30 dc).

Rounds 6–7: crochet without inc.

Round 8: inc 5 dc evenly spaced around (35 dc).

Round 9: crochet without inc.

Round 10: as Round 8 (40 dc).

Round 11: crochet without inc.

Round 12: as Round 8 (45 dc).

Round 13: crochet without inc.

Round 14: as Round 8 (50 dc). This is the widest part of the head – adjust your marker thread!

Rounds 15–19: crochet without inc.

Round 20: dec 5 dc evenly spaced around (45 dc). This is nearly the back of the head.

Round 21: crochet without dec.

Round 22: dec 5 dc evenly spaced around (40 dc).

Round 23: crochet without dec.

Round 24: as Round 22 (35 dc).

Round 25: crochet without dec.

Round 26: dec 10 dc evenly spaced around (25 dc). Do not break the yarn tail!

Stuff the head evenly with approximately 16 g (½ oz) stuffing material.

To close the head, crochet 1 dc into every 3rd dc until the opening is closed after approximately 5 rounds. The sheep's fleecy wig will cover this area later.

Body

Yarn A, crochet hook 3.5 mm (US E/4).

To determine the position of the neck count 11–12 rounds from the nose towards the back of the head and mark the spot with a white pencil. Starting at this spot, draw a circle, approximately 5 cm (2 in) diameter.

Round 1: Insert the hook into a gap around this circle between stitches, pull up a loop and work as a dc. Crochet 18 dc around the circle. This step is quite tricky; you will need to twist the hook back and forth to manoeuvre the thick bouclé wool through the yak wool. Take care to always crochet around the outside.

Now switch to crochet hook 8 mm (US L/11).

Round 2: inc 6 dc evenly spaced around (24 dc) to make the shoulders.

Rounds 3–5: crochet without inc.

Round 6: inc 3 dc evenly spaced around (27 dc).

Rounds 7–8: crochet without inc.

Round 9: as Round 6 (30 dc).

Rounds 10–14: crochet without inc. This is the plumpest part of the sheep.

Round 15: dec 3 dc evenly spaced around (27 dc).

Round 16: crochet without dec.

Round 17: dec 5 dc evenly spaced around (22).

Round 18: as Round 17 (17 dc). Leave a tail of yarn hanging.

Stuff the body with approximately 40 g (1 ½ oz) stuffing material.

Close the opening with a separately crocheted bottom disc. This will allow the sheep to sit well, and you can also open it again later for re-stuffing after washing if necessary (see p.18). Using yarn A, follow the instructions for 'Elephant's head' on p.23 to Round 3 (18 dc). Ss last stitch for a neat finish.

Sew the disc neatly into the opening.

Fleecy wig

Yarn A, crochet hook 8 mm (US L/11).

Rounds 1–6: follow the instructions for 'Elephant's head' on p.23 to Round 6 (36 dc).

Rows 1–4: crochet 13 dc to one side of the disc and dc 4 rows, to make a rectangle for the neck.

Legs (x 4)

Yarn A, crochet hook 8 mm (US L/11).

Round 1: starting at the thighs, ch 15 and join with ss to make a ring.

Rounds 2–6: dc 5 rounds (15 dc).

Switch to yarn B and crochet hook 3.5 mm (US E/4).

Round 7: inc 6 dc evenly spaced around (21 dc).

Rounds 8–14: crochet 7 rounds without inc – the 1st leg is finished!

Make 4 small discs for the sheep's *hooves*, following the instructions for 'Elephant's head' on p.23 to Round 3 (18 dc). Sew the hooves neatly to the lower leg openings.

Stuff all 4 legs lightly, particularly sparingly at the openings so the joints are nice and loose. Stroke the opening flat and sew closed.

Ears (x 2)

Yarn B, crochet hook 3.5 mm (US E/4).

Follow the instructions for 'Elephant's head' on p.23 to Round 2 (12 dc).

Turn the small circle over and crochet a row of 6 dc. Crochet 10 rows.

To finish, dc all the way around the ear.

Eyes (x 2, 2 discs each)

Use thin white yarn and crochet hook 2.5 mm (US C/2).

To make the white of the eye, ch 3, join with ss to form a ring, crochet 10 dc into the ring – finished.

To make the pupil, ch 3 with dark brown yarn, join with ss to form a ring and crochet 6 dc into the ring to make a slightly smaller disc.

Sew the pupil to the white of the eyes with brown thread.

Finishing

To fit the sheep's fleecy *wig*, smooth it to the head, remove, apply fabric glue sparingly and pin it back on head. The wig and body wool should meet at the neck (see bottom right).

There are 8–9 rounds between the fringe (bouclé) and the tip of the nose (yak-merino). The corners at the temples are the perfect spot for attaching the ears. Sew the wig in place with small tight stitches right around, best with a double thread and twice around. Back, head and neck are connected firmly together.

To position the front *legs* at the side of the body, imagine a line running straight down from the temples. Attach the legs to this line, 1 dc down from the neck, with approximately 11 cm (4 ¼ in) between the legs, measured horizontally across the chest.

Mark the positions determined and apply fabric glue to the leg seams. Press the legs to the body and attach with pins.

Position the back legs on the same imaginary vertical line at the same height as the sheep's bottom, to allow the animal to sit straight.

Sew all 4 legs in place with a double thread and twice around.

Make a small fold in the *ears* and sew to the temple corners.

Embroider French knot *nostrils* (see p.14) with brown yarn just beside the first round if the nose, approximately 1 cm ($^3/_8$ in) apart.

The *eyes* are positioned to the left and right, approximately 3 rounds above the nostrils and approximately 4 cm (1 ½ in) apart.

To make the eye sockets, take a strong thread and sew through the face several times between the marked eye points. Then sew the thread in well. At the same time as making eye sockets you will have made a slight nose ridge, which gives the face shape and expression.

Apply a drop of fabric glue to the back of the eyes, press into the sockets. Sew in place with small stitches.

Embroider a *mouth* with 2 straight stitches approximately 3 rounds under the nose.

Crochet the *tail* using yarn A: ch 8 and dc 1 row. Use the yarn tails to attach it to the centre of the sheep's bottom.

Small Animal Friends

Chameleons

Chameleons are one of the most fascinating creatures in the animal kingdom. Not only can their telescopic eyes swivel independently and their long sticky tongue shoot out quickly to catch prey – to remain undiscovered, some of them can take on the colours of their surroundings.

You will need

- Approximately 25 g (1 oz) green merino wool, for example Lang Merino 120 (yardage: 50 g/120 m or 130 yds) (yarn A)
- Small amount of coloured wool, for example sock wool with flecks (yardage as above, if necessary double yarn) (yarn B)
- Thin green (a different shade from yarn A) sock wool, baby wool, or cotton yarn, for example Schachenmayr Catania (crest and mouth) (yarn C)
- Approximately 18 g ($^{2}/_{3}$ oz) unspun sheep's wool or polyester filling for stuffing (see p.18)
- 2 small wax beads
- Green thread, needles and pins
- Fabric glue if using (see p.18)
- Crochet hooks 3.5 mm and 2.5 mm (US E/4 and C/2 or B/1)

Crochet technique: double crochet (dc) (US single crochet), chain stitch (ch)

Tension/gauge: 28 dc x 26 rows = 10 x 10 cm (4 x 4 in)

Measurements: approximately 27 cm (10 ½ in) high and approximately 6 cm (2 $^{1}/_{3}$ in) long

Body

The chameleon is mostly crocheted using yarn A, but work coloured stripes or spots as you choose using yarn B. Starting at the tip of the tail, crochet in rounds with crochet hook 3.5 mm (US E/4).

Round 1: ch 3, join with ss to form a ring and crochet 6 dc into the ring to make a small circle.

Rounds 2–30: dc 29 rounds (6 dc).

Round 31: inc 2 dc evenly spaced around (8 dc).

Round 32: crochet without inc.

Round 33: as Round 31 (10 dc).

Rounds 34–41: as Rounds 32 and 33 for 8 rounds (18 dc).

Rounds 42–47: inc 2 dc into every round (30 dc).

Rounds 48–53: crochet without inc.

Round 54: dec 4 dc evenly spaced around (26 dc).

Round 55: as Round 54 (22 dc).

Round 56: crochet without dec.

Round 57: dec 2 dc (20 dc).

Round 58: as Round 57 (18 dc). Do not break the yarn tail yet!

Stuff the body loosely with approximately 15 g (½ oz) stuffing material. Do not stuff the tail, but stuff the tail base loosely ensuring the transition from stuffed to not stuffed parts is gradual.

Now crochet the last round: dec 4 dc (14 dc). This is the neck. Sew the yarn tail in well.

Head

Round 1: ch 3, join with ss to form a ring and crochet 6 dc into the ring. This forms the nose.
Round 2: 2 dc into every stitch (12 dc).
Round 3: crochet without inc.
Round 4: 2 dc in every 2nd dc (18 dc).
Round 5: crochet without inc.
Round 6: 2 dc in every 3rd dc (24 dc).
Round 7: crochet without inc.
Round 8: 2 dc in every 4th dc (30 dc).
Rounds 9–14: crochet without inc.
Round 15: dec 10 dc evenly spaced around (20 dc).
Round 16: as Round 15 (10 dc).

Now stuff the head lightly.

Attach the head and body, making sure the yarn changes are hidden on the under side of the belly.

Flatten the stuffed openings, apply fabric glue very sparingly to the edges and press the parts together tightly, holding them in place with pins.

Sew the head and body together with a double thread, using very small stitches and twice around. Flatten the under side of the belly and pinch the back to make a spine.

Legs (x 4)

Ch 3, join with ss to form a ring and crochet 8 dc into the ring to make a small circle.

Crochet 18 rounds to make a tube. Do not stuff the legs!

Crochet the opening closed while making 2 *toes*: ch 4, dc 1 row (4 dc), dc this ch to the leg opening (see left). Make the 2nd toe in the same way.

Eyes (x 2)

Using yarn A, ch 3, join with ss to form a ring and crochet 8 dc into the ring. Crochet 1 round – finished.

Pull the start yarn very tight to close the hole and sew the yarn tail in. Sew a small bead to the centre of each eye, if you choose (see left).

Horn

Ch 14, join with ss to form a ring and dc 2 rounds.

Then dec 2 dc in each 2nd round until you have a point. Sew the yarn tail in well.

Stuff the horn with a little wool so it stands up. Press the opening together with two fingers and push one side inwards and upwards to make a slight angle, which will make the horn point backwards.

Finishing

Angle the *horn* so it tilts backwards (see above). Apply fabric glue very sparingly to the base and press it to the back of the head near the neck. Pin in place until the glue is dry. Sew with a double thread, twice around.

Roll the tip of the *tail* up tightly approximately 4 cm (1 ½ in). Glue in place before sewing to take the pressure off the sewing thread.

Fold the front *legs* approximately in half with the joint pointing backwards (see left).

Fold the back legs with the joint pointing forwards and slightly upwards by making the lower leg a fraction longer than the thigh.

The front thighs start at the neckline and the back thighs start at the tail base. The legs and

belly should touch the ground when the animal is standing.

Apply glue to the joints and very sparingly inside the legs too, press tightly and pin in place until the glue is dry. Carefully sew with a double thread.

Attach *eyes* to the side of the head approximately 7 dc apart. Glue, pin and sew in place. Use dark thin embroidery thread and straight stitches to embroider around the eyes.

Embroider a chain stitch line for the *mouth* using yarn C.

Dc a line from neck to tail using yarn C and crochet hook 2.5 mm (US C/2) as a base for the *crest*.

To make the spikes, start at the neck: dc 2, ch 3, dc into the 1st ch, then 3 dc – one spike is finished. Continue in this fashion to the tail base, making the spikes smaller towards the tail and using the photos as a guide.

Guinea Pigs

Many children would love to have a little guinea pig to hug and play with, but guinea pigs don't necessarily like being held. However you can cuddle a crocheted guinea pig as much as you like!

You will need

- Approximately 12 g (1/3 oz) sock wool or baby wool in black and white (yardage: 50 g/210 m or 230 yds)
- Some mohair/silk mix yarn for fluffiness, for example Schulana Kid-Seta (see p.17) (optional)
- Small amounts of thin sock or baby wool in pink (inner ear, paws, mouth) and brown (eyes)
- Approximately 5 g (1/4 oz) unspun sheep's wool or polyester filling for stuffing (see p.18)
- White, black and pink thread, needles and pins
- Fabric glue if using (see p.18)
- Crochet hook 2.5 mm (US C/2 or B/1)

Crochet technique: double crochet (dc) (US single crochet)
Tension/gauge: 28 dc x 28 rows = 10 x 10 cm (4 x 4 in)
Measurements: the finished animal is approximately 10 cm (4 in) long

Head

Crochet in rounds, changing colour between black and white as you prefer.
Round 1: ch 3, join with ss to form a ring and crochet 6 dc into the ring.
Round 2: 2 dc into every dc (12 dc).
Round 3: 2 dc into every 2nd dc (18 dc).
Round 4: 2 dc into every 3rd dc (24 dc).
Rounds 5–10: crochet without inc – the head is finished!

Pull the starting yarn tight so there is no hole. Sew in the yarn ends.

Body

Follow the instructions for the 'Head' to Round 4 (24 dc).
Round 5: 2 dc into every 4th dc (30 dc).
Rounds 6–9: crochet without inc.
Round 10: inc 6 dc evenly spaced around (36 dc).
Rounds 11–19: crochet without inc.
Round 20: dec 6 dc evenly spaced around (30 dc).
Round 21: crochet without dec.
Round 22: as Round 20 (24 dc). This is the neck.

Lightly stuff the body and head and sew them together very neatly with double thread.

Ears (x 2)

Ch 3, join with ss to form a ring and crochet 6 dc into the ring. Turn and crochet 1 dc into every dc to form the outer ear.

Inner ear (x 2): use pink yarn to ch 3, join with ss to form a ring and crochet 5 dc into the ring. Sew to the outer ear with pink thread.

Legs (x 4)

Using pink yarn, ch 3, join with ss to form a ring and crochet 8 dc into the ring – the pink paw is finished.

Change to your chosen fur colour and dc 3 rounds.

Pull the start yarn tight to close the hole and sew in all yarn ends.

Finishing

First, sew the small *ears* in place. Position them near the neckline approximately 2 cm (¾ in) apart. Pin to the head and, when satisfied with the positioning, apply fabric glue sparingly to the edges and press to the head. Later sew them on tightly with thread using very small neat stitches.

Embroider a cross for the *mouth* using pink yarn or embroidery thread, over Round 1 of the nose (see above).

Embroider 2 French knots (see p.14) for *eyes*, approximately 2 cm (¾ in) apart and with 5–6 dc between the eyes and mouth.

To finish, attach the *legs*. Position the front legs 2 rounds from the neckline and spaced 2–2.5 cm (¾–1 in) apart. Position the back legs along the same line as the front legs, approximately 3.5 cm (1 ⅓ in) apart. Apply fabric glue, pin the legs in place and ensure the guinea pig can stand firmly. Then sew on well using small stitches.

Ducklings

Playful ducklings like to be in a group so crochet a whole flock of them. They make a great decoration for an Easter table.

You will need

- Approximately 10 g ($1/3$ oz) yellow 100 % merino wool, for example for example Austermann Merino 105 (yardage: 50 g/ 105 m or 115 yds) (yarn A)
- A small amount of thin orange sock wool, baby wool or cotton yarn, for example Schachenmayr Catania (feet and beak) (yarn B)
- Yellow eyelash yarn, optional (head tuft) (see p.17)
- Brown yarn (eyes)
- Unspun sheep's wool or polyester filling for stuffing (see p.18)
- Needle, thread and pins
- Fabric glue if using (see p.18)
- Crochet hooks 3.5 mm and 2.5 mm (US E/4 and C/2 or B/1)

Crochet technique: double crochet (dc) (US single crochet); half treble crochet (htr) (US half double crochet); treble crochet (tr) (US double crochet); picots
Tension/gauge: 22 dc x 22 rows = 10 x 10 cm (4 x 4 in)
Measurements: approximately 8.5 cm (3 $1/3$ in) high

Head

Yarn A and crochet hook 3.5 mm (US E/4).
Rounds 1–3: follow the instructions for 'Guinea pig's head' (see p.83) to Round 3 (18 dc).
Rounds 4–8: crochet without inc – finished!

Pull the start yarn tight to close the hole and sew in all yarn ends.

Body

Rounds 1–4: follow the instructions for 'Guinea pig's head' (see p.83) to Round 4 (24 dc).
Rounds 5–10: crochet without inc.
Round 11: dec 3 dc evenly spaced around (21 dc).
Round 12: crochet without dec.
Round 13: dec 3 dc evenly spaced around (18 dc).

Stuff the head and body loosely and sew them together with thread using neat stitches.

Wings (x 2)

Ch 10, then crochet back along the chain as follows: 1 ss, 1 dc, 2 htr, 1 dc (centre).

Continue in mirror image: 2 htr, 1 dc, 1 ss – this makes half the wing.

Ch 1 and work the other half in the same fashion: 1 ss, 1 dc, 2 htr, 1 dc etc.

Tail

Ch 6, then dc in rows without crocheting the edge stitches to make a triangle.

Beak

Yarn B, crochet hook 2.5 mm (US C/2).

Ch 8, now crochet back along the chain as follows: 1 ss, 1 dc, 1 htr, 1 dc, 1 ss – this makes half the beak.

Ch 1 and continue crocheting in mirror image on the other side of the chain: 1 ss, 1 dc, 1 htr, 1 dc, 1 ss.

Fold the beak in half, point to point – finished!

Feet (x 2)

Yarn B, crochet hook 2.5 mm (US C/2).

Round 1: ch 3, join with ss to make a ring and crochet 6 dc into ring.

Rounds 2–4: crochet without inc (heel).

Round 5: 2 dc into every dc (12 dc).

Rounds 6–8: crochet without inc.

Fold and flatten the tube, which will be crocheted closed using dc, forming the toes using picots while doing so: ch 3, crochet 1 dc into the 3rd ch from the hook and 1 dc in the next dc to anchor (double layered) – one toe is finished. Work 3 toes evenly spaced and crochet through both layers when anchoring.

Finishing

Position the *wings* at the side of the body at the neckline. Apply glue to the top of the wings only so they remain free to move, and sew on firmly using thread and small stitches.

Now attach the *beak*. Fold it in half, apply fabric glue to the fold and press to the face, leaving a nicely rounded forehead. Pin until the glue is dry, then sew on with small stitches.

Embroider French knots (see p.14) for *eyes* with dark brown yarn.

To make the *head tuft*, crochet 4 dc or ss with eyelash yarn to the top of the head.

Sew on the small triangular *tail* with fabric glue using small stitches.

Apply fabric glue to the *feet* and press to the body, close together. Due to its large feet the animal should be able to stand easily. Sew in place once the glue is dry. Your first duckling is finished. Now continue with numbers 2, 3, 4...

Squirrels

Children love to spot squirrels hopping about in the forest. Squirrels have even been known to plant beautiful trees by accident when they've forgotten where they've buried their winter food store.

You will need

- Approximately 20 g (¾ oz) reddish brown merino wool (yardage: 50 g/164 m or 180 yds) (yarn A)
- Eyelash yarn (red, orange or brown) (tail and ear tufts)
- Small amounts of thin black and pink yarn (eyes and mouth)
- Unspun sheep's wool or polyester filling for stuffing (see p.18)
- Needles, thread and pins
- Fabric glue if using (see p.18)
- Crochet hook 2.5 mm (US C/2 or B/1)

Crochet technique: double crochet (dc) (US single crochet)
Tension/gauge: 30 dc x 32 rows = 10 x 10 cm (4 x 4 in)
Measurements: the finished animal is approximately 8 cm (3 in) high

Head

Yarn A, crochet hook 2.5 mm (US C/2).
Round 1: ch 3, join with ss to make a ring and crochet 6 dc into the ring. This makes a small circle for the nose.
Round 2: 2 dc into every dc (12 dc).
Round 3: crochet without inc.
Round 4: 2 dc into every 2nd dc (18 dc).
Round 5: crochet without inc.
Round 6: 2 dc into every 3rd dc (24 dc).
Rounds 7–11: crochet without inc.
Round 12: dec 4 dc evenly spaced around (20 dc).
Round 13: crochet without dec.
Round 14: as Round 12 (16 dc).

Stuff the head loosely and crochet the opening closed, with 1 dc in every 2nd dc.

Body

Crochet the body directly onto the stuffed head. Remember that this time the head rounds run vertically, while all the other animals in this book have horizontal rounds for head and body (see left).
Round 1: insert the hook into the neck, pull up a loop and work 15 dc around.
Round 2: 2 dc into every dc (30 dc).
Rounds 3–12: crochet 10 rounds without inc.
Round 13: inc 4 dc evenly spaced around (34 dc).
Rounds 14 and 15: crochet without inc to make a round tummy.
Round 16: dec 6 dc evenly spaced around (28 dc).
Round 17: crochet without dec.
Round 18: as Round 16 (22 dc).

Round 19: crochet without dec.
Round 20: dec 8 dc evenly spaced around (14 dc).

Stuff the body lightly and crochet closed in the same way as the head.

Front legs (x 2)

Rounds 1–2: follow the instructions for 'Head' to Round 2 (12 dc).
Rounds 3–12: crochet 10 rounds without inc – finished!

Back legs (x 2)

Rounds 1–7: follow the instructions for 'Front legs' to Round 7 (12 dc).
Round 8: inc 4 dc evenly spaced around (16 dc).
Rounds 9–12: crochet without inc.
Round 13: dec 5 dc evenly spaced around (11 dc)

Stuff all 4 legs loosely and sew closed with thread.

Tail

Round 1: ch 3, join with ss to make a ring and crochet 8 dc into the ring to make a small circle. This is the tip of the tail.
Round 2: 2 dc into every dc (16 dc).
Rounds 3–20: crochet without inc.

Sew the opening closed with thread.
To make the tail fluffy, crochet all the way around it using eyelash yarn.

Finishing

To attach the *front legs*, apply textile glue sparingly to the edges and press the legs to the sides of the body at the neckline. Pin in place until dry, then sew on using small stitches and thread.
Attach the slightly fatter *back legs* at the same level as the bottom. Make sure the animal can sit firmly without tipping over before sewing in place.

Position the lower (sewn) edge of the *tail* at the same level as the back legs and the squirrel's bottom, so it sits well.
To attach the tail, apply fabric glue to the lower edge and to approximately 3 cm (1 in) of the lower tail (avoiding the eyelash yarn), press to the back, pin and then sew.
Fold back the tip of the tail to make a nice outward curve.

Embroider a small cross with pink yarn directly over the 1st head round (tip of the nose) to make the *nose* and *mouth* simultaneously.

Crochet the fluffy *ears* directly onto the head, approximately 8 rounds up from the tip of the nose and 1.5 cm (½ in) apart. Insert the hook into a gap between stitches and crochet 4 new dc using yarn A. Crochet 2 rows yarn A and 2 rows eyelash yarn. Sew the yarn tails in well.

Embroider 2 French knots (see p.14) for *eyes* using black yarn, approximately 3–4 rows up from the nose and approximately 2 cm (¾ in) apart. Finished!

Frogs

These small green frogs are lively and fun. You can also hide a surprise gift in their flexible mouths.

You will need

- Green merino wool, approximately 10 g (⅓ oz) each (yardage: 50 g/105 m or 115 yds) (yarn A)
- Yellow merino wool, approximately 10 g (⅓ oz) each (yardage: 50 g/105 m or 115 yds) (yarn B)
- Pink yarn (mouth) (yarn C)
- Thin sock wool, baby wool or cotton yarn, for example Schachenmayr Catania, in a different shade of green (eyes, lips) (yarn D)
- As above in yellow and orange (eyes)
- Unspun sheep's wool or polyester filling for stuffing (see p.18)
- Needles, thread and pins
- Fabric glue if using (see p.18)
- Crochet hooks 3.5 mm and 2.5 mm (US E/4 and C/2 or B/1)

Crochet technique: Double crochet (dc) (US single crochet), slip stitch (ss), picots
Tension/gauge: 24 dc x 24 rows = 10 x 10 cm (4 x 4 in)
Measurements: the finished animal is approximately 7 cm (2 ¾ in) long and 6 cm (2 ⅓ in) high

Head and body

Make 2 identical discs for the head and body, using yarn A (back) and yarn B (stomach), crochet hook 3.5 mm.

Round 1: ch 3, join with ss to form ring and crochet 6 dc into the ring.
Rounds 2–7: follow the instructions for 'Elephant's head' on p.23 to Round 7 (42 dc).
Round 8: crochet without inc – 1 disc is finished!

Mouth

Crochet a 3rd pink disc using yarn C, as above to Round 7.

Back legs (x 2)

Round 1: using yarn A ch 3, join with ss to make a ring and crochet 4 dc into the ring.
Round 2: crochet 2 dc into every dc (8 dc).
Rounds 3–17: crochet without inc.
Rounds 18–19: inc 2 dc evenly spaced around for 2 rounds (12 dc).

Stroke the tube flat and close the opening with dc, working 3 picots as toes: ch 3, crochet 1 dc into 3rd stitch from hook, then 1 dc into both layers of the tube – the 1st toe is finished. Ch 3 again and repeat as above until you have 3 toes.

The legs remain unstuffed.

Front legs (x 2)

Follow instructions for 'Back legs' to Round 5, closing as above with dc and picot toes.

Eyes (x 2)

Yarn D, crochet hook 2.5 mm (US C/2).
To make 2 small half-spheres for the protruding eyes, ch 3, join with ss to make a ring and crochet 8 dc into the ring to make small circle. Dc 1 round – finished!

Finishing

Place the green and yellow discs right sides facing and crochet together along the edge using over 30 ss. Sew the yarn ends in well.

Turn right sides out and stuff the *body* very loosely.

Fold the pink *mouth* disc in half and push it into the opening of the yellow-green body. Position the disc accurately, opening the mouth wide if necessary to pin everything in place.

Crochet the lips around the mouth using yarn D and crochet hook 2.5 mm (US C/2). Insert the hook through both layers (green or yellow layer and the pink disc) to join the mouth to the body.

Continue with the long *back legs*. Fold the foot and toes to the front, then fold the leg in half (see photo p.94). Apply a tiny drop of fabric glue to the knee joint and press until the glue is dry.

Position both legs at the side of the body, approximately 10 dc apart measured around the back where green and yellow discs meet. Make sure the frog can sit securely. Angle the mouth upwards. Pin in place and correct until you're satisfied.

Apply a drop of fabric glue to the inside of the thighs, press them to the body and pin. Sew everything, including the joints, in place well with thread using small stitches.

Position the *front legs* under the yellow stomach approximately 6 dc apart, 3 rounds up from the back legs and 4 rounds down from the mouth. The forward-bent feet should touch the ground.

Apply glue sparingly to the edge of the *eyes* and press in place, approximately 3 rounds from the mouth and 2–3 dc apart. Stuff the eyes before attaching them if desired. Pin until the glue is dry then sew in place with thread using small stitches.

To finish, embroider the eyes using yellow chain stitch and add an orange French knot (see p.14) to the centre.

Owls

This owl collection is made from leftover sock wool – so you can see which colour socks my loved ones wear!

You will need

- Approximately 25 g (1 oz) sock wool in your chosen colour (yardage: 50 g/210 m or 230 yds) (yarn A)
- Orange, yellow, white and dark brown yarn (eyes and beak) (yarn B)
- Leftover eyelash yarn, colour to suit the body
- Approximately 12 g ($1/3$ oz) unspun sheep's wool or polyester filling for stuffing (see p.18)
- Thread, needle and pins
- Fabric glue if using (see p.18)
- Crochet hooks 3.5 mm and 2.5 mm (US E/4 and C/2 or B/1)

Crochet technique: double crochet (dc) (US single crochet); treble crochet (tr) (US double crochet); half treble crochet (htr) (US half double crochet)
Tension/gauge: 20 dc x 22 rows = 10 x 10 cm (4 x 4 in)
Measurements: the finished animal is approximately 10 cm (4 in) high

Head and body

Double yarn A, crochet hook 3.5 mm (US E/4).
Rounds 1–4: follow the instructions for 'Elephant's head' on p.23 to Round 4 (24 dc).
Rounds 5–6: crochet without inc.
Round 7: inc 3 dc evenly spaced around (27 dc).
Round 8: crochet without inc.
Round 9: as Round 7 (30 dc).
Round 10: crochet without inc.
Round 11: as Round 7 (33 dc).
Round 12: crochet without inc.
Round 13: as Round 7 (36 dc).
Rounds 14–20: crochet without inc.
Round 21: dec 10 dc evenly spaced around (26 dc).
Round 22: crochet without dec.
Round 23: dec 6 dc evenly spaced around (20 dc).

The head and body are finished – stuff evenly.

Bottom

Follow the instructions for 'Head and body' to Round 3 to make a disc (18 dc).

Sew the bottom disc in place using thread and neat stitches.

Wings (x 2)

Ch 12, 1 ss in last ch, then 1 dc, 3 htr, 1 tr – this is the centre. Continue in mirror image: 1 tr, 3 htr, 1 dc and 1 ss.

Crochet 1 dc turning stitch and crochet the same on the other side: 1 ss, 1 dc etc. – one wing is finished.

Outline with eyelash yarn for fluffy wings.

Eyes (x 2)

Single yarn B, crochet hook 2.5 mm (US C/2). Make the eyes out of 3 different sized discs.

Large eye disc (yellow or white):
Round 1: ch 3, join with ss to make a ring and crochet 10 dc into the ring.
Round 2: 2 dc into every dc, ending the round with ss.

Medium eye disc (orange):
Round 1: ch 3, join with ss to make a ring and crochet 6 dc into the ring.
Round 2: 2 dc into every dc.

Small eye disc or pupil (dark brown):
Ch 3, join with ss to make a ring, and crochet 8 dc into the ring – finished!

Place the eye rings over each other. Apply a tiny amount of fabric glue and press together. Sew tiny stitches around each disc.

Beak

Ch 6 with orange yarn (same as medium eyes). Crochet in rows. Do not crochet the last stitch of each row to make a small triangle. Leave yarn tails long.

Ears (x 2)

Double yarn A, crochet hook 3.5 mm (US E/4).
Ch 5, then follow the instructions for 'Beak'.
Crochet a few strands of eyelash yarn to the tips.

Finishing

Position the *ears* at the side of the head approximately 8 rounds apart. Apply a drop of fabric glue, press the ears to the head and pin. Sew on with thread.

Position the *wings* 2 rounds down from the ears. Apply fabric glue sparingly to the top of the wings, press to the body and pin. Sew in place.

Position the finished *eyes* approximately 6 rounds down from the 1st row with the discs touching each other. Sew to the head using a darker yarn and visible stitches (see left).

Position the *beak* just below the eyes. Apply a little fabric glue to the back of the beak, pinch between thumb and forefinger to shape, then glue and pin in place. Sew on using orange yarn. Sew the beak yarn tail into the body.

Crochet 1 round around the *bottom* disc using eyelash yarn – the owl is finished!

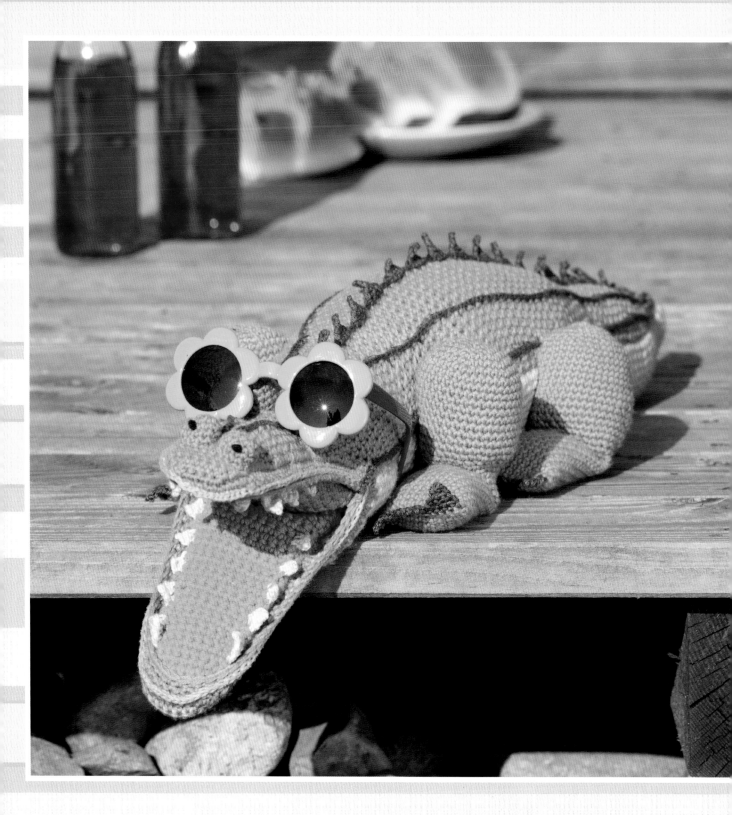

Acknowledgements

A famous German fashion designer once said in an interview, 'My ideas always create a lot of work for my colleagues…'

    I borrow this statement boldly but in all modesty, and my heartfelt thanks go to all the wonderful people who edited, arranged, corrected, photographed and printed the books. Particularly Maria A. Kafitz and Bianca Bonfert (editorial and design) and not last Ulrike and Jürgen Pfeiffer (styling and photos).

Angelika Wolk-Gerche

Magic Wool Fairies
Christine Schäfer

Creative Felt
Felting and Making More Toys and Gifts
Angelika Wolk-Gerche

Weaving With Children
Ute Fischer

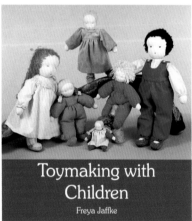

Toymaking with Children
Freya Jaffke

Crafts Through the Year
Thomas and Petra Berger

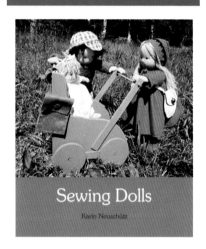

Sewing Dolls
Karin Neuschütz

Making Soft Toys
Karin Neuschütz

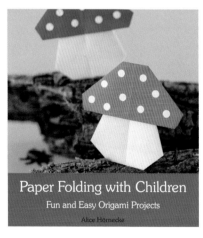

Paper Folding with Children
Fun and Easy Origami Projects
Alice Hörnecke

Beautiful Paper Stars
Craft Decorations for Every Season
Ursula Stiller, Armin Täubner and Gudrun Thiele